THE PROGRAM DIRECTOR'S HANDBOOK

BY BOB PAIVA

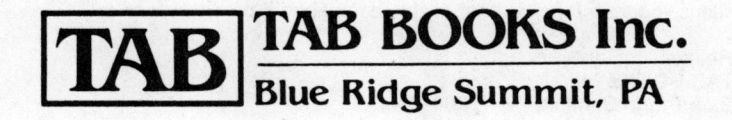

TAB BOOKS Inc.
Blue Ridge Summit, PA

FIRST EDITION

FOURTH PRINTING

Printed in the United States of America

Reproduction or publication of the content in any manner, without express permission of the publisher, is prohibited. The publisher takes no responsibility for the use of any of the materials or methods described in this book, or for the products thereof.

Copyright © 1983 by TAB BOOKS Inc.

Library of Congress Cataloging in Publication Data

Palva, Bob.
    The program director's handbook.

    Includes index.
    1. Radio broadcasting—Handbooks, manuals, etc.
I. Title.
PN1991.55.P34   1983   384.54′02′02   82-19364
ISBN 0-8306-0373-8
ISBN 0-8306-1363-3 (pbk.)

TAB BOOKS Inc. offers software for sale. For information and a catalog, please contact TAB Software Department, Blue Ridge Summit, PA 17294-0850.

Questions regarding the content of this book should be addressed to:

    Reader Inquiry Branch
    TAB BOOKS Inc.
    Blue Ridge Summit, PA 17294-0214

Contents

Preface: Programming—Art, Science, or Craft? iv

1 The Program Director 1
Basic Daily Duties of the P—The PD and the Daily Log—Hiring, Motivating, Training, Firing—Communicating with Your Boss

2 On the Air 9
What Makes a Disk Jockey Tick?—Radio News—The Newsjock—Establishing Rapport with the Audience—Contests—Hot Clocks—What Is Personality?

3 Promotion 38
Off-Air Promotion—General Rules for Off-Air Promotion—Some On-Air Promotion Ideas—Remote Broadcasts as a Promotion Tool—How to Get Good PR for Your Station—Registration of Words, Trademarks, and Identifying Slogans—Things to Keep on File

4 Music 54
A Sample Music Selection Policy—Formula for Computing the Number of Records You Should Play—Basic Music Research Techniques—Music Business Terminology

5 Research and Surveys 66
Survey Techniques—Understanding ARB—What Listeners Do While They Listen—Lifestyle Research—Population Pattern Changes

6 The Public Responsibility 94
Audience Acceptance and Public Service—The Lottery Law—Handling Complaints—The Ombudsman

7 Random Observations 103
Thoughts on Success—Ask Me—Pitfalls to Avoid—Computers in Programming

Appendix Interviews on Successful Programming 110
Ken Wolt—Don Berns—Gene Taylor—Terry Young—Clark Smidt—Tom Shovan

Index 161

Preface: Programming
—Art, Science, or Craft?

When approaching the study of broadcasting, the first determination to be made is whether we shall consider programming as an art, a science, or a craft. In making this determination we will set forth some of the conditions of the study.

If we determine programming to be a:

—*Science*, then it follows that we can assume there to be present certain "laws" of science. We can evaluate specific programming against these criteria and make judgments based on scientific comparison.

—*Art*, we take a much more subjective view of the subject. In a recent court case (City of Hartford against a sculptor hired by the city to create a sculpture for the park in front of City Hall) the court seems to have held that "art is whatever the artist says it is." Art has certain forms, but it has no circumscribed parameters. Unlike scientific study, art cannot be reduced to "laws" of science.

—*Craft*, we will have neither science nor art but an entity without the laws of science nor the freedom of the arts. We will have a *craft*, an interpretative rather than creative concept.

Perhaps the first question in seeking an answer to our problem is whether programming is "creative" or "interpretative."

I think we could immediately agree that not all program material is creative. Certainly a great deal of the material that is broadcast is not only lacking in creativity, but in interpretation as well. Much of what we hear is imitative. Imitation is a fact of life in every form, artistic or scientific. It has no bearing on the discussion.

Is the essence of programming creative? My feeling is that programming itself is a most creative process. It is a process of observing and assimilating the culture in which it thrives. It is a process of utilizing the combined product of experience to create a form of expression and information that is different from all of the individual parts of its creation. The process of programming is creative and therefore I believe should be considered an *art*.

Within the process of programming there is contained an element that we might call the "mechanics" of programming. The mechanics are the forms and structures we use to quantify the creative process. This part of programming is not creative; it is entirely interpretative. It is not an art, it is a craft.

An adequate analogy might be found in the theater. In a play, the writing is considered creative. It is art. The acting is interpretative. It is a craft. In radio, we might say that the programming is creative and the program interpretative.

Can programming be reduced to scientific laws? There are elements in the creative process which can be quantified into scientific fact. Those elements revolve about the part of the process involved with the observation and assimilation of the collective experience.

We can research attitudes. We can research opinions. We can establish models against which behavior can be measured and compared. We can define the behavioral study to a point where it is considered a science.

What cannot be quantified into behavior models is the process of assimilation, digestion, and interpretation of this information. It is my contention that this process is the essence of the creative element in programming.

Were we able to quantify programming into scientific laws, it would be possible to research information, apply that information to the laws of programming, and develop programs with infallible audience appeal.

What we have is a rather different situation. In a graphic art, the creative process and the craft mesh into a final form. That form may be viewed and it is possible to research opinions on the final form. We can determine what the viewer likes or dislikes about the graphic.

In exposing the listener to a program, the listener can make judgments regarding the final form. We can apply scientific research techniques to determine likes and dislikes with regard to what was heard.

It is not possible in either case to determine opinion in advance. No one really knows what the painting will look like until it is finished—not even the artist himself. No one really knows what the program will be like until it happens. It is within the nature of the program that when it happens . . . it's gone. The minute the piece of programming exists, it fades and is replaced the next instant with another piece of programming. Every radio station, every piece of programming, every minute of the broadcast day is getting better ... or worse. Change itself is the only constant.

Scientific measurement in either the graphic or audio mediums can be applied only to the past. The future is yet to be created.

To maximize the art of programming, utilization of science and craft are important. The science of examination, measurement, and quantification must be entwined with the interpretative craft to provide the elements from which the creative process springs.

If we believe that programming is an art, we must also believe in the subjectivity of that art. Subjectivity is part of art. *Art is whatever the artist says it is.*

What about the reactive nature of programming? Does this interfere with the creative process? The fact that programming reacts to the socioeconomic climate does not affect the process. The absorption of the surrounding climate, reflected in music, sculpture, and painting makes those creations no less. It is the ability of the programmer to absorb the surrounding elements and the process by which those elements are forged into the program message which constitute the creative process in broadcasting. Reaction provides the raw material about which the process functions. This reactive quality is quite unlike the interpretative quality found in a craft.

The art of programming differs from the program material. The material may be a product of scientific development and craft skills. The art is in the process.

Chapter 1
The Program Director

One of the most exciting things that can happen to a program director (PD) in radio happens every day. He turns on the radio station and is treated to a mirror image of himself. The PD hired the announcer, told him what to say, and sometimes how to say it. He had a hand in just about everything that comes out of the speaker. The radio station is a mirror image of his personality. Whatever he is, however he sees himself, will be reflected in that mirror.

Viewed from other perspectives, the program director's influence seems more limited than it is. A record promotion man sees the program director's most important responsibility as choosing the music the station will play. To the people on the air, the PD is seen as a combination boss, wailing wall, father confessor, and shrink. To the station manager, the PD is the guy who is always bucking the sales department, who overprotects his air people, and who is riding a fine line that may blow the license any minute.

The program director may see himself as the guy in the middle—the bridge between all of the elements that make the station function smoothly.

As I see it, there are two ways to approach the job of program director. In the first situation, the PD sets himself up as the arbiter of all disputes with regard to sound, commercial quality, music, and personalities. The station is organized on a chain of command function like the Army. The PD sets the rules and his "team" follows. He's like a football coach.

This technique has proven exceptionally successful for a number of major radio programmers. This PD may utilize hot lines, "bat" phones, rules, and formats. The staff is controlled in part by fear and in part by respect. The station has a highly structured, orderly sound.

The failure of this system is its inability to develop people. It does not encourage experimentation. It does not encourage thought. The system produces PDs capable only of perpetuating the system. Few have shown the ability to extend beyond it. This style of program director is administrative rather than managerial.

The second style puts the program director in the same position as a motion picture director. His job is to develop a set, a script, and a series of scenarios which will be interpreted by the actors. This PD chooses the music, sets format guidelines and coaches the performance.

To illustrate the difference, we might draw from TV. Given a specific set of directions, think how differently the execution would be if played by Peter Graves in *Mission Impossible* and then by Peter Falk as *Colombo*—the same set of directions, the same actions, two entirely different interpretations.

Imagine how different two radio stations would sound as two jocks, just as varied in their approach, handled the same set of music and format elements. Multiply this variance in conception and execution five or six times and you can see how distinctively different the two radio stations would sound.

I much prefer the second aproach when I work. It allows people to grow and develop their own styles. It allows the station to be flexible to immediate situations, to be more reactive to nuance and subtlety. It is one of the basic functions of the program director's responsibility to develop his people, to give them the tools to grow and the room to grow.

Within this framework, the PD has the opportunity to put his stamp on the product. He can mold it, bend it, and love it. Because the station is so much a reflection of himself, the program director takes rejection by the audience personally. This personal factor makes radio the program director's medium.

BASIC DAILY DUTIES OF THE PD

Monitor: Listen to the station. Check out every daypart, every day.

Comment: Comment to each jock about his show. Compliment or critique as needed. Call the all-night man just to let him know you're listening. Air personalities equate your comments with caring.

Act: Correct errors immediately. Your failure to act may translate as your failure to care.

Create: Every day come up with new ideas to make the sound fresh. Design new promotions, discuss new public service campaigns, sell lines, freshen commercial copy, review the music.

Involve yourself with your people: Talk to your jocks, engineers, sales people, and news people. Talk about personal things. Do not let relationships become casual.

Get input: Ideas and constructive criticism can come from anywhere. Encourage others to provide you with ideas. Seek critiques on your sound from people you respect.

Be aware of the competition: If you can't listen, get somebody to do it for you. A new promotion, a new air personality, a news "scoop" by the competition can hurt you if you're not aware of it.

Involve yourself in the community: Encourage communication with your station by civic groups, charity organizations, schools, and government. Get out of the station and be seen at some of their meetings. Be visible. Make your news people and personalities visible. Your station can't be part of the community if your people are not part of it.

Be positive: Negative attitudes destroy morale. It's your job to keep morale up by keeping attitudes positive. Encourage excellence, compliment success, be there to help when someone fails.

Share: Share your thoughts, your plans, your ideas. Get your people involved with the station and where it's going.

Review your goals: Every day you need to look at everything that's done in terms of whether it has contributed to your goals. If it hasn't, change it.

Set an example: Follow the rules you've set for others.

Be cost conscious: Encourage your staff to do the same. Dollars are precious. Savings in wasted time and materials translate into profits. Profits may translate into raises and other rewards.

Do something: Every day, let your people know you're working, you're interested, and you care.

THE PD AND THE DAILY LOG

Perhaps the most important single document in the radio station is the daily program log. Until recent deregulation, the station was not permitted to broadcast without it. Although no longer required by the federal government, there are still a number of good reasons (such as accurate billing) to maintain a program log.

The log contains information relevant to the station's committment as indicated in the license with regard to news, public affairs and religion. The log is the PD's responsibility. To exercise that responsibility, the PD must personally oversee the following tasks.

Pre-broadcast check: Examine the log daily to see that it carries all of the elements it should. Are all news, public affairs, public service, and commercial elements entered properly?

If the station is demographically targeting commercial content, the PD will want to check that the commercial content is relevant to the daypart. Commercials carrying irrelevant information can be switched by the sales manager to more relevant positions. This benefits both the station and the client. If the station limits commercial content in some hours, the PD will want to check that those limits are not exceeded.

Post-broadcast check: When the log is completed, the PD will want to check it over before it goes to accounting. Things to look for are air personality signatures on each page, proper sign-on, sign-off where needed, exact time notations or other with regard to commercials and proper logging of news.

Monthly commitment check: Each month the PD should call for a week of log days. These logs must then be examined to add up the exact minutes of news, public service, religion, and other actually performed during the sample of seven weekdays. That examination should be compared against the station's FCC license promise to make sure the commitment is being fulfilled. If it is not, changes can be ordered immediately. A report to management should be filed each month on the results of this inspection.

HIRING, MOTIVATING, TRAINING, FIRING

The personnel aspects of the program director's job divide into a number of areas. For purposes of our discussion we have divided them into hiring, motivating, training, counseling, shielding and firing.

Hiring: The demand for qualified air talent exceeds the supply. Yet the supply of available talent far exceeds the demand. The operable word in aligning supply with demand is *qualified*. Program directors spend a lot of time looking for talent. Although they may not have immediate openings on the staff, each likes to keep a "talent pool" available to call on. PDs spend time listening to airchecks submitted by candidates for employment. They may travel to listen to air personalities who have not applied but in whom they may be interested.

In the interview, a great deal of attention may be paid to the character of the candidate. In a business as close as radio, the determination of how well the candidate will fit into the existing staff is important. Many a talented performer has been passed over because he wouldn't fit in, or would disrupt the harmony of the existing staff. Has the candidate a reputation for being difficult? Do you think you can control him? How do you feel his personality will relate to your audience? These questions may play as big a part in the hiring procedure as the candidate's demonstrated air talent.

Motivating: Being behind a microphone for hours every day is tedious, humdrum work. The glamour of the business soon fades in the pressure cooker of the broadcast studio. Consistent performance requires a high degree of concentration and alertness. Part of the PD's job is to help the air personality maintain concentration and to motivate him past the "blahs" when they creep into his performance. Even the most skilled performers often find the routine a depressant and may begin to reflect this attitude without being aware of it. The PD has to be alert to spot this tendency and do something about it.

Praise, encouragement, and reassurance are all good techniques for motivation. The air personality is insulate from audience reaction. Unlike a stage actor, he has no audience to play to or against. He operates in a vacuum. The program director functions as a surrogate audience by responding to his performance. Reassurance builds confidence and confidence motivates good performers to be better.

Money (in the form of raise or bonus) may be used for motivation but the true performer does not perform just for money. For the true performer, pride is a deeper, more satisfying reward than money. Money makes a better reward than it does a motivation.

You must help your people to perform well because they *want to* and not out of fear of reprisal. In answer to my question regarding motivation one major program director indicated that he motivated his staff "by allowing them to keep their jobs." Fear is the motivational technique he uses. I think it is fair to say that this particular executive usually programs stations with high personality turnover and that few of his people have gone on to great careers of their own. Fear ruined their pride of accomplishment. Fear heightened their sense of insecurity. Fear is *not* a good technique for motivation.

Training: A new air personality needs to be told what is

expected of him. An old air personality needs to be coached on fine-tuning the performance. Training is a never-ending process.

Air people are usually encouraged to listen to airchecks of their own performances and to think about how they could have performed better. The PD may sit in on these critiquing sessions. Some stations have group sessions in which air personalities critique each other.

The group procedure has some inherent dangers. Intra-staff rivalries and bitterness may result from these encounter sessions. The exercise could prove counterproductive and is not recommended.

The best technique seems to be to have the PD and the personality review an aircheck and see if it meets the goals of the station.

In some situations the PD may provide no critique at all. Personalities are left to fend for themselves. A "shape up or ship out" attitude prevails.

In training, rules must be clear. Objectives must be spelled out. Responsibility must be assigned. Critique can then be directed to specific points. "Errors" can be evaluated. While the rules must be firm, the requirements of discipline must never blind human values. New avenues of expression must be allowed to develop in order to maximize the training experience.

Counseling: Air personalities are sensitive, insecure people. They have often been uprooted from familiar situations and relocated in strange cities among unfamiliar people. They need someone to talk to in confidence. That person is often the program director.

The PD's door should be open and his ear available for a discussion of personal problems. The confidentiality of those discussions must be assured. Sympathetically listening to problems can go a long way toward establishing rapport and inspiring loyalty among staff members.

Shielding: This is sort of an unofficial function. The nature of his job means that the PD often acts as a buffer between the air staff and management. Air personalities are subject to pressures from the job and from the audience. Without protection from these pressures, tension builds and performances decline. Shielding the performers from outside influences while giving the complainants a fair hearing puts the PD in a difficult position. Taking the heat is part of the job.

Firing: One of the least favorable and most difficult tasks the

PD has is firing. Firing implies mistakes made in hiring, or failures in training, or unwillingness to cooperate.

Sometimes firings result from no real fault on anyone's part. They may be a product of a change in program philosophy. Whenever dismissal is for anything other than due cause it is part of the PD's human responsibility to see to it that the firing causes the least inconvenience possible to both the employee and the station. When possible, the PD should try to help relocate the talent.

In a small staff situation, it is impossible to remove yourself from the personal considerations of any firing and hold yourself "at arm's length." An employee let go (for other than good cause) may not fit into your format but may be perfectly suited to another. You should give him the opportunity to find out.

Hiring, training, motivating, and firing are all part of the day-to-day operations of the station. These personnel functions and how they are handled are a most important factor in developing loyalty and maintaining morale. One rule that seems to work is "everyone does not need to be treated equally but everyone must be treated fairly." Your people deserve the best judgment you have to offer on matters that affect their personal lives.

COMMUNICATING WITH YOUR BOSS

For many PDs, the communication problem with the general manager is at a minimum—there is no problem because there is no communication. Often in these situations we read about the program director who got let go because of "policy differences" between the GM and the PD. They had an argument before they had a discussion and the PD lost.

Many general managers expect PDs to be order takers— execute the orders, stay out of the line of fire, and you'll last a long time. In these stations the manager is often heard to complain that he can't delegate authority. He can't get away from his desk because he doesn't have people to whom he can delegate authority and responsibility.

Obviously, here is a weak manager. He can't accomplish the first step in management. He can't relieve himself of minor duties in order to concentrate on the overall picture. The program director who finds himself in this situation must, for his own sanity, make an attempt to develop communication with the GM.

In order to have meaningful communication, certain elements must be present:

Recognition that everybody has strong points and weak points:

Trading one person for another in a job simply readjusts the weakness, it does not solve the problem. You must enter the relationship with a commitment to the proposition that you are going to help the people you've got be better. You are going to work with management to make their strong points stronger and help your people develop strength in their weak areas. Establishing this kind of thinking means that the GM won't be looking to fire somebody every time a person has a problem. You'll both be looking for ways to help your people grow and maximize your potential.

Listening: Most communication fails because somebody didn't listen. Listen to the other side of the discussion. In listening you may find points to strengthen your own position.

Candor: You are working together. Both parties must be candid about their thoughts and opinions. If you can't speak openly, you can't communicate.

Candor is the most difficult stage of discussion. Failure to achieve candor will be recognized by both parties as failure to achieve true consensus.

Commitment: When a decision is reached, both parties must be committed to it. Failure to commit to the decision reached will seriously damage attempts to resolve communication problems.

Solving internal communications problems with your boss is a matter of creating an atmosphere of mutual understanding of the job that needs to be done, a commitment to doing it, and the freedom to express yourself on how it can best be done.

Chapter 2
On the Air

We in radio are often guilty of being bad teachers.

Broadcast educations usually do not deal in the realities of the broadcast career—the back-stabbing, the throat cutting, the rate-cutting, the deals and the trades necessary to get the job done on a day-to-day basis.

Some schools have misled students to believe that they can idealistically expect freedom to exercise creativity, and to be handsomely paid for that privilege. What exists, in fact, are routine assignments and low pay scales. Broadcasters are constantly being faced by recent graduates who have been led to believe that they will have creative control over music, copy, commercials, and news. In fact, they will be greeted by music lists, formulas, prescribed copy lines, commercial logs and controlled newscasts.

Applicants are led to believe that there are thousands of job opportunities awaiting them in the field when, in fact, the industry can absorb only a small percentage of the flow of graduates.

If education, creativity, and opportunity are not the real world, what is?

Education: In a study conducted by Fredrick Jacobs of Michigan State University in 1974 the following was determined. I do not believe the percentages have altered significantly since the study was taken.

Of 869 radio station managers polled, more than half (50.3%) expressed an unfavorable attitude toward hiring college-educated students. Another 33.1% claimed neutrality while only 16.5% responded positively. It was felt by a large majority of the managers that college-educated communications students didn't understand the realities of commercial broadcasting. Education *per se* is not an entree to broadcasting although education should not be discounted. We will return to this theme later.

Pay scales: The average starting pay for announcers and/or newsmen is something on the order of $175—$200 per week. By 1980 economic circumstances, the starting salary is low compared to many non-broadcast opportunities. The starting salary of broadcasters is highly subject to the laws of supply and demand and the supply is such that if you don't want the job at those rates, somebody else does.

Creativity: It is within the nature of the commercial, competitive radio business today to utilize creativity as a programming tool designed to attain specific audience goals. With that in mind, certain elements of the programming may be developed with specific audience appeals in mind. These elements usually include items such as music mix, air personalities, conversation patterns, commercial positioning within the hour, and news composition and delivery. The creativity of the air personality today is to be found in his ability to organize and deliver these elements in a manner which the audience will perceive as "fresh." An old saying is that the way to tell a good disk jockey from a bad one is to give them the same records and the same format and see what each does with it.

Women and minorities: There is no question that opportunities for women and minorities in radio were once limited. Due to pressure by the federal government, those opportunities have opened up considerably. It would be naive, even at this date, to assume that the new opportunities for women and minorities have come with the willing cooperation of radio managers. Considerable prejudice still exists. Legislation designed to force affirmative action in these areas have been required to open some of the doors.

Minorities tend to be viewed as "assets" more regularly than women. The high visibility of minority pressure groups has created a situation in which the hiring of minorities may be viewed by management as necessary to relief of minority hiring pressures.

Women still face a problem in establishing themselves as viable air personalities. Although there have been some successful women air personalities, I know of no case which can be documented to prove that a station gained appreciable audience because it had a woman on the air nor lost any appreciable audience when the woman was replaced by a man. Given the success of so many male radio performers (Bill Balance, Dr. Don Rose, etc.), the reverse cannot be said to be true. This does not predict a negative pattern for women in broadcasting. What it does say is that women have yet to find their particular identity on the air. The role model in radio for a long time was exclusively male. Many female air personalities initially adopted the delivery and style which had become identified with the male broadcaster. The potential for women will be reached when the stereotype is broken and the unique quality women bring to the air can be developed.

Voice: While, in an audio medium, a good voice is a considerable asset, a good voice will not guarantee a future in broadcasting. It is generally accepted that a good voice backed by a good education will vastly improve chances at success. The value of a solid educational background cannot be underestimated. The successful air personality must have the sensitivity to absorb the situation around him, the intelligence to analyze and collate these feelings and impressions, and the education to verbalize himself in a creative manner. Education is the best way to develop these facilities.

What about off-air positions? For every on-air position in a radio station, there are approximately six off-air positions, ranging from management to secretarial. Perhaps the most important contributions off-air are made by sales. It is generally accepted that to be a radio time salesman requires no previous knowledge of radio. Familiarity with the medium is an advantage but not a requirement.

Sales is an area where many people who set out to get on the air find solid radio careers. The ability to sell, to persuade, to convince, and to close is a unique one not limited by racial or sexual considerations. In that sense, sales is a "pure" area of radio. It is a fact that most radio salesman make as much or more money than air personalities. The sales job is not as subject to variations in rating results and so provides an element of stability. The competition is rough but the rewards are commensurate. Those who sell harder get paid more. That cannot be said for the on-air positions.

What about talent? As in any creative field, talent is a welcome ingredient. However, talent is not an easily definable quality and a performer who is rejected as "untalented" by one director may find himself hailed as a genius by another. Talent is as much a situation of timeliness and willingness to capitalize on opportunity as it is an inner quality of the performer.

In a business which I have characterized as cut-throat competition, talent itself may not be the determining factor of success. I would not place an inordinate degree of concern on one's perception of his/her own talent. Desire to succeed and willingness to survive are often as important to success as talent.

I realize that I have, to this point, sounded rather negative on the subject of a career in broadcast. If the business is hard, competitive, often not financially rewarding, unstable and frustrating, why have I chosen it as my career? Why have so many people sought to become broadcasters?

For those of us who become broadcasters there is no other career which can bring the feeling we get from getting behind the mike. Broadcasting is an emotional release for us.

For some, broadcasting will bring rewards of fame, recognition, and wealth. For those for whom these rewards will not be forthcoming there is an intangible known as "satisfaction." For some, the audience is a force that brings with it a renewal of our energy levels. We are insecure, obsessed people who find expression in an insecure, obsessed profession.

The question of why we become broadcasters is moot. It's the only thing we can do . . . and be happy.

WHAT MAKES A DISK JOCKEY TICK?

The radio station air personality, the disk jockey, is the most complex element of the program cycle. The complexity exists not just because he/she is a person, but because he/she is a special *kind* of person. Programming a radio station creatively requires an understanding of this complex personality.

What is this mystique, this personality trait that leads everyone including perfect strangers to accept and even take a liking to this person? It is their natural facility as "wooers." These are people who have an inherent flair for winning acceptance of others. This attribute, more than any other single factor, enables them to gain entree.

Unfortunately, on the other hand, many of these "wooers" have what psychologists call "infantile personalities;" they have failed to grow up emotionally. This perhaps appears to be a damaging statement. However, paradoxical as it may seem, what is clinically a personality "defect" is often a great asset. Usually these are persons in whose early backgrounds an adequate degree of love and security has been missing. They have never been quite able to believe that anyone can really love or want them. To compensate for this, they have a compulsive need to win and hold the acceptance and affection of others. Hence they have acquired great skill in "selling themselves" to everyone. The "wooer" is often basically passive and dependent, with an insistent, constant craving for love and acceptance which he needs to provide the support and reassurance he requires.

When such a person is subjected to the slightest depreciation, his anxieties and feelings of worthlessness are aroused. Hence he tends to react with anger and a sense of rejection and to set out to "get even."

They may be openly subordinate because of the need to exhibit superiority. They are neither willing nor able to conform to . . . procedures . . . established for them, nor to cope with such personal problems as excessive drinking, financial troubles, gambling, domestic difficulties, or entanglements with women.

The ability to win this initial acceptance through "wooing" is the mystique that distinguishes many outstanding from the merely good or mediocre. While many men are excellent technicians, they lack the sensitivity and empathy of the "wooer" which makes the difference between merely good and outstanding performance.

Reread the preceding five paragraphs. You will probably recognize yourself. You'll certainly recognize somebody you know in the entertainment industry. Yet all of these comments weren't written about actors, musicians, or disk jockeys. They were adapted from a book entitled *How to Build a Dynamic Sales Organization* (R. McMurray, Ph.D., J.S. Arnold, McGraw-Hill 1968). This is a most valuable book for any manager or PD because successful salesmen are very much like successful performers. They are highly motivated people who pour great energy into their job. They possess great self-confidence, although derived from feelings of inadequacy and inferiority. They have a driving need for recognition and the rewards of money, status, and prestige. In short, they are people willing to face the competitive challenge.

It is the job of the successful manager to take this fund of energy, motivation, and spirit and channel it. That's what makes a disk jockey tick—motivation and management.

RADIO NEWS

Radio news does not play a *dominant* role in the life of the average American. This is not to say that radio news does not play an important part in American lives, nor is it to imply that radio news cannot be a major asset to programming. It does mean that since radio news plays a diminished role in our lives, radio news must be structured in a different way to make it important.

The average American family today gets its basic news orientation from television. Studies of TV rating books show a marked increase in adult audience during TV prime time access news periods and again at 11:00 p.m. Television's ability to deliver both words *and* pictures, plus its new-found ability to cover with immediacy, have helped television surpass newspapers as our major source of news information. Video tape, minicams, and satellite transmissions have revolutionized TV news and the American perception of it.

Newspapers still retain a major position in news by their ability to do in-depth coverage. In spite of the failure of many newspapers to weather the competitive battles, newspapers, especially in major metropolitan markets, remain a favorite and powerful source of news.

Radio is at best a tertiary news information source for most people. For many years, news departments (especially in pop-oriented radio stations) were relegated to minor status. News was considered an intrusion on the broadcast hour, imposed by promises made to the FCC at license renewal.

Recently, with the aging of the audience as the World War II "baby boom" population passes into middle age, radio has become more interested in attracting "adult" audiences. With that change has come a new respect for news as a programming element. There have been many changes in radio news over the past few years. Let's look at some of them.

Writing style: For most of us, our initial contact with news was in written form. We read it in the newspaper. The style was constructed for reading. When read aloud it was stilted, formal, and not in concert with the way we spoke or were spoken to. Few people speak in perfectly constructed sentences. Most people speak in phrases.

Radio newsmen recognized the need for a new writing style. It was the advent of television news and television "happy news" styles that forced radio newsmen to react.

Most of the great early radio newsmen had print backgrounds. Although they wrote their scripts for speaking, their styles of delivery and the content of the newscasts still reflected the formal Who/What/When/Where style of reporting found in newspapers. As television news began to rely on visual impact there was less need for complete information in the written presentation. Reporting could be cut down to introduction, comments, and close. The pictures told the story.

Although radio couldn't do it the same way, radio had to adapt to the TV writing style. Sentences became shorter. Stories were cut to include just basic facts. Headline news carried more stories in less time. Pacing became a factor in presentation. "Action" news became a byword—deliver a lot of information quickly. Radio writing styles were permanently altered.

Delivery style: Initially, radio news delivery styles depended on "authoritative" delivery. The newsman delivered facts and stories. His rate was steady, his delivery firm and assured.

Competition changed all that. Today's radio newsman uses pacing, inflection, pause, and emotion as basic elements of his delivery. Happy stories are delivered with a lilt, sad stories seriously. Radio news that grabs audience attention today is "performed," not just delivered. The essential emotional value of the story is apparent in the delivery.

Content: Prior to the advent of television, in a time when parts of our country were insulated from the world community, it was the responsibility of radio news to bring the world to the people. Today there is no section of the country to which major national and international events are not flashed instantaneously by satellite television broadcast. The world comes to the people; the world community has shrunk. Consequently, radio news has changed. Today radio news has a "people orientation." The important message is not just what happened, but how it affects the individual listener.

Pocketbook stories usually lead our interest. Stories about inflation, energy costs, interest rates, and housing catch our immediate attention. The content of the story is meant to show how each of these items affects the individual's pocketbook. A rise in $x\%$ in wholesale meat prices will add how many cents to the steak you buy?

In a smaller world community, stories about other people are interesting. We know that the world is so small that what happens to others can happen to us. Stories about tragedy, illness, cures, and show business catch our ear. They are "people-oriented" stories. People—the "you" orientation has been the big change in radio news.

Verbiage: We've seen a world in which the use of words clouds where it should clarify. We are told people *interface* in business when we mean they *had a meeting*. People aren't *killed* anymore, they are *fatally wounded*. A *morale program* today is described as *implementation of various motivational programs for internal staff.*

In radio news, if the audience doesn't understand what you've said, you haven't said it.

Careful consideration should be given to the vernacular of the audience and the vernacular of the target audience in particular. "Today the police apprehended an alleged assailant who fatally wounded a shopkeeper last evening" is not the same as "Today the cops caught the guy who murdered the owner of XXX cafe yesterday."

To be effective, news must be understood. News is an informational, not an educational, process.

Demographic orientation: News has the capability of adding to the programming by tailoring the demographic appeal of the editorial content of the newscast. To do this, two facts must be ascertained: The existing potential audience demographic, and the target demographic the station seeks to attract.

There's not much sense in delivering stories appealing to 34-49 year-old men if there are no 34-49 year-old men available to radio at that time of day. You must have some idea of whom you wish to appeal to and have some idea of the demographic appeal of each story. For example; in morning drive the station's target may be adult men. Stories about sports, money, traffic, automobiles, finance, and action stories about crime might be significant. Mid-day, the emphasis might be switched to women. Show business, consumer stories, and family-oriented items might have major appeal here. For afternoons, celebrity stories, action news, sports, weekend weather forecasts, and stories about entertainment available that night might be pertinent. By nighttime, TV has grabbed the bulk of the adults. "Sex, Drugs, and Rock & Roll," as the song says, may be topics of interest to younger audiences. Stores about music celebrities may take the headline position.

The idea is simple: Who is there to hear it? Who do you want to attract to hear it? Who do you serve with it? These are good questions to ask when demographically constructing a newscast.

Investigative journalism: Long an entity reserved for newspapers, investigative journalism has become a major part of radio and television news. In investigative journalism, Who/What/When/Where is only a part of the story. The important story element is *Why?* If the incidence of teenage alcoholism has risen, there is a reason for it. What is that reason? When the question arises, the responsive radio news team seeks out the answer.

Investigative reports on topics of community interest make a major contribution to programming.

On-the-scene reporting: If budget and staff size permit, there is no substitute for an "outside" reporter who is on the scene at major news happenings. Having your own man there to get "exclusive" coverage is very important. On-the-scene reporting brings immediacy to the news. People hear it as it happens. Having your own man on the scene shows your community that you care, that you are involved. If you have the budget to afford news vehicles, make sure they are highly visible at news events. They give you "presence."

If you can't afford an outside man, make extensive use of telephone cross-index and reverse-index listings. Obtain firsthand reports on the phone from neighbors in the vicinity of the event. This technique can place you at the scene without leaving your desk.

Voicers: One of the best ways to add pacing, inflection, and drama to a newscast is to make extensive use of "voicers." Voicers play the same role in radio as film does in TV. Illustrating your story with other voices on tape, interviews with participants, comments from people on the scene, or phone reports from field reporters add "size" to your news department. You seem bigger than you are. Audio can capitalize on the "theater of the mind" concept, bringing the audience to the event.

Using voicers is not difficult. You will require a resourceful reporter, a telephone, a good tape deck, a good tape editor, a cartridge playback system, and a little time.

Audience involvement: Giving the audience an opportunity to express its opinion on the news of the day has long been a feature of radio news. Television has now adopted this feature and regular broadcasts on CBS-TV feature listeners sounding off. Obtaining audience participation is easy. All you have to do is ask for it, tape record incoming calls, select interesting comments and provide a spot in the news where comments can be played back. Providing access allows the audience to become involved. It says you care.

Radio news does not offer the visuals available in TV. Radio news does not offer the in-depth coverage of the newspaper. What radio news can offer is *immediacy*. We can do it *now*, when it's happening. Even if all we have available is a telephone we can take the listener to the scene. We can offer *relevance*. We can show the listener how the news affects him.

To be an asset to programming, radio news must provide information in a way that holds listener interest. Newsmen must understand the auditory senses. They must understand the stimuli of pacing, inflection, style, pitch, and loudness as elements of delivery. *Relevant content interestingly delivered* is radio news today.

THE NEWSJOCK

For five, eight, or ten minutes every hour the contemporary radio station switches operations to the newsroom. We have discussed how news can be a contributing element to station programming. Now let's look at how the newsperson can become a more integral part of that presentation.

Once we looked for *newsmen*. Today we look for *newspersons*. Understanding that news can be demographically targeted has led to major news opportunities for women. The growth of consumerism has meant the addition of women on the theory that women are more attuned to the day-to-day consumer function.

Once the newsroom was the exclusive preserve of whites. News was presented by white newsmen for consumption by white audiences. Minority news was given minor reportage and most often gained status only when it involved tragedy. Today there are not only a significant number of minority newsmen to be found but there is a significant amount of news coverage devoted to news of interest to minority communities. As rating services improved their techniques, minorities became a major part of the "rated" audience. In seeking to gain those audiences, radio used news as one point of appeal.

Even the definition of the term "minority" has changed. Minorities now being served include not only those based on color but those of national origin, lifestyle, and sex. Black news, Puerto Rican news, Indian news, women's news, and news devoted to the gay community are featured in many areas.

Once radio news looked for journalists. Today's radio demands more. Today's radio demands a newsperson who is conscious not only of the content of the news but of its audience appeal. I term this newsperson the *newsjock*.

Where once "authority" was the essence of delivery, another dimension has been added. This new dimension was the product of television. John Cameron Swayze on NBC-TV brought news to television in the '50s with a breezy delivery, a well-tailored look, and a carnation in his lapel. CBS-TV countered with the boyish good looks of Douglas Edwards. The competition heated when David Brinkley added wry comments and Walter Cronkite created a friendly, empathetic delivery.

News on the radio was slow to change . . . and died. People turned to television as their main source of news information. Radio news became an intrusion into the airspace rather than an attractive element of programming.

Radio has finally begun to catch up and the newsjock is the product of that change. The newsjock handles news as a disk jockey handles records.

Perhaps the best practitioner of the newsjock style is Paul Harvey. A Harvey newscast is not only "all the news that's fit to print" but "all the news that fits ... we print." News stories, many chosen for their demographic appeal, are delivered in a style geared to specific audiences and "jocked" to whisper, to shout, and to cry.

I remember one Paul Harvey newscast when, after delivering the news of the day, Paul ended the newscast with a story about the death of his pet dog. It was a warm, human story that added great depth to the newscast and softened the negative effect of the war news that preceded it. I remember being brought to the verge of tears at his story and his delivery. That's the newsjock—the newsman who makes the story reach out and touch the audience on a personal level.

I believe the day of the radio journalist who does not understand the philosophy of jocking the news is numbered. The day of the program director who feels he can allow five, eight, or ten minutes of his broadcast hour to go without keying it to his demographic is gone.

Newsjocking is not news management. Our consideration is not editorial. Our consideration is stylistic. The *newsjock* is one of the new phenomena of contemporary radio.

ESTABLISHING RAPPORT WITH THE AUDIENCE

Audiences react to performers to whom they relate. Bing Crosby is reputed to have said that the secret of his success lay in the fact that the average guy, singing in the shower, felt he could sing as well as Crosby could. There is a message in that comment for programmers.

In establishing rapport with the audience, you must bring the station to the audience and bring the audience to the station.

Relate: Think "you" and "your." Information and conversation should be with the listener's point of view in mind. What does the listener need to hear? What information does the listener need to hear? What information does the listener need? What in your comments will enlighten, inform, or entertain the audience?

One of the top programmers in the country, Dan Clayton, gave it a name. He called it "significant trivia." Most talk on the radio is trivial. Your trivia should be significant to some point the audience can relate to, or it shouldn't be on the air.

Avoid "inside" conversation about the station or things to which the bulk of the audience has no frame of reference.

Vulnerability: It means that you are capable of being wounded. This is a new concept in the entertainment arena and one that has found immediate acceptance in the theater. The concept of the "star" who is beyond reach has been replaced by the performer the audience can touch. Audiences don't expect you to be perfect. They expect you to be human. The TV comedy team that breaks up during a sketch may be seen as fallible and human, not as imperfect.

Vulnerability can be a tool. I can remember when Woody Roberts, a very talented morning man who has since moved into management, made purposeful mistakes on his program. Listening to Woody's program was like driving down a highway lined with billboards. Suddenly you come across a billboard with a large hole punched in it. *That's* the billboard you remember, the one with the hole. The purposeful error is like that billboard. It causes the audience to stop and be aware.

There is a danger. Driving down a highway lined with billboards with holes punched in them is an ugly sight. Similarly, listening to a radio program with a lot of errors is an uncomfortable experience. Woody used the purposeful error as a way of demonstrating his vulnerability, his human quality. Everybody makes an occasional mistake. The audience can relate to it.

Inform: Most people listen to the radio to be entertained. However, they need to be informed. Those needs, not met, will soon become apparent and the audience will switch to the station that fills that need.

On a snowy day a mother may listen to the radio for music but she needs information on how to dress her child for school. Information bits that relate to audience needs surround the audience with a blanket, a feeling of security. They say you care.

Honesty: Don't offer what you don't intend to deliver. Asking for requests you don't intend to play will demonstrate that you really don't care. When you don't know, say so. Honesty is a key to audience rapport. Note the success of country formatted radio stations in attaining rapport with the audience. This is a major element in their ability to be believed. It's called honesty.

Entertain: Sell the "sizzle" as well as the steak. Communicate entertainment in your performance. Don't just play the records . . . *sell* them. Don't just read the commercials . . . *sell* them. You are doing what you are doing for your audience. Make them know it. Show you care.

CONTESTS

Contesting has been a part of competitive commercial programming almost since the inception of the form. Originally designed to test audience response, contests were used not by the stations but by the sponsors to evaluate reaction to commercial messages.

As audience measurement became a part of competitive radio, stations turned to contests as a method of inspiring audience response, and as a measure of audience size and activity. The ability to get results for a client was a measure of radio's effectiveness. The ability to draw audience reaction was demonstrated by the number of cards or letters stations could garner from contests.

In some markets, contesting became so expensive that stations who won the contest ratings battle often lost the financial profit battle on the bottom line. Audiences began looking forward to contests as much as to music or information. The powerful "greed" motivation had entered the picture.

Inside the station, contests are viewed with a slightly jaundiced eye. We'll look at how some areas of the station see contesting in a different light:

Contesting to the programmer: A programming tool needed to attract and hold audience attention.

Contesting to the manager: A bottom line expense item a necessary evil.

Contesting to the sale department: A sales tool; a "talk" piece; a sponsor tie-in.

Contesting to the station lawyers: A way to lose the license; a breeding ground for FCC/FTC problems.

Let's take a more detailed look at these attitudes about contesting.

Programming: In addition to attracting audience attention, a contest may provide the station with a focal point—a tangible item around which to program. It gives the air personalities something new to talk about. It gives the station a vehicle to promote. It provides a theme around which to design outside promotional material.

Contests provide an opportunity for the programming department to sell its own people. It shows the staff that the station is competing. It energizes their attitudes about their station. Contests provide a working ground for the programmer to involve himself with the sales department.

One of the standard tricks of the trade in the automobile

business is to hold audience promotions. Many times the dealer isn't attempting to attract new customers as much as he is working to show his own salesman that he's competing.

Management: Contesting costs. In a well-run radio station, the promotion/contest budget will run at least 10% of the station's gross revenue. However, contesting is a normal business expense. We tell our clients they should spend 10% of their income on advertising. Contesting is our method of advertising. We use our medium to promote ourselves.

Sales: Contests provide the sales department with a new talking point, something they can approach a client with to show the "excitement" on the air. It gives them a unique selling point from which to work. Many times a client tie-in to a promotion is the lever needed to make the sale. It gives the salesman a "gimmee" to sweeten up his pitch. Giving away some of the client's product in a contest may add impact to his purchased schedule.

A warning: If the "gimmee" is part of the sales package, you may have to log the giveaway commercial. Check with your lawyers. It depends on whether the "giveaway" was part of the sales pitch and a condition of the sale.

Legal: A recent case in which an improperly conducted contest resulted in the loss of a station license has made legal staffs very critical of contesting. Considerations with regard to contests and rating book "hype" must also be taken into account.

Certainly, improper contesting can cause great problems for the station. A great deal of care in contest design, rules, and execution is needed. Properly run contests provide no danger to the station.

If you have any question about a contest, call your lawyer and run the question past him. If he doesn't know the answer right away, he'll sound out somebody at the Commission and give you the probabilities on how the Commission would rule if a problem developed.

Audience: Contesting provides the audience with many benefits. They like the fun of it; they like winning. Contesting gives the audience a reason to sample new stations. It gives the audience a reason to become exposed to a station. Contesting gives the individual an opportunity to participate, to become part of the programming. Contesting provides an opportunity for fantasy fulfillment—the chance to win something valuable. In the audience's perception, a contest says "thank you for listening" from the station.

To review: Contests provide a focus for talk and promotion.

Contests provide an excitement ingredient and a talking point for sales. Contesting provides a tool for the station to reach out for the audience and involve them with the station.

Contests say "I love you."

HOT CLOCKS

Among the most carefully kept programming secrets in radio is the program director's *hot clock*. The hot clock is, in essence, the format broken down into graphic form and depicted on a clock-like graph. Each format and/or music element may be so illustrated.

In this section we shall look at examples of both format and music hot clocks. The examples are not meant to be definitive of the hot clock design for every pop station. They are, however, examples of hot clock designs which I have successfully programmed several radio stations.

In designing a station hot clock, several programming elements must be determined in advance:

- ☐ Will this program hour carry news? If so, how much? five minutes, ten minutes?
- ☐ Will the newscasts carry commercial spots? One minute per cast? One and a half?
- ☐ How many minutes and/or units of commercial time must be accounted for on the clock?
- ☐ What other program elements will you decide to include?
Weather? Station promo lines? Contests?
Public service announcements? Time checks?
Traffic?

The most important element in the design of the hot clock is the placement of the commercial spot announcement. Because of their nature, commercials are often perceived by the audience as an intrusion on the broadcast hour. Although we will see in another chapter how this intrusion can be lessened by demographic spot placement, we must always be conscious of the fact that the major reason most of the audience has tuned in the radio is music. Any interruption in the music flow may be considered an intrusion.

Although it is quite common today to find commercial spot loads of eight minutes on music stations, our examples will deal with commercial loads of 10-14 minutes per hour. I think it can be predicted that as spot costs maximize and station income potential levels out, most stations will increase their spot loads to the 10-14 minutes levels in order to increase income potential.

For purposes of definition we will use two terms in discussing spot load and placement. They are *spot* and *unit*. They will be used somewhat, but not entirely, interchangeably. A *spot* will usually refer to a commercial of :60, :30 or :10 second length. A *unit* will refer to one spot, regardless of length. Therefore we will usually refer to a two minute spot load as containing three units. This spot break may be two :60 second spots, a :60 and two :30s; or a :60, a :30 and a :10. It could even be three :10 second spots. Consequently a two minute spot break may or may not actually fill two minutes of air time.

Some ground rules: When talking about spot breaks we will limit all breaks to two minutes maximum/three units. Many experiments have been carried on with regard to extension of the spot cluster to three minutes/four units. (two :60s, two 30s) or of selling commercial announcements only in :60 configurations in an effort to maximize dollars and minimize intrusion.

My experience with these experiments has been that television spot breaks, of seemingly unrestricted units, have become so annoying that spot breaks on radio of longer than two minutes/three units are perceived as having the same intrusive quality as television spots. Since radio listeners are not bound by story lines and visual impact, long spot breaks encourage tuneout.

While the sale of only :60 spots is an advantage to diminishing the perceived intrusion of the two-minute/three unit spot break, it is unrealistic to confine the station sales department in this way at a time when spot costs make it more feasible for clients to purchase :30 second units.

Another ground rule of spot placement revolves around a concept known as *quarter hour maintenance*. This is a phenomenon created by the methodology of ratings services. The theory concerns the following observation: One person, listing his listening time to a particular station as any five-minute period during any specific 15-minute period of the broadcast hour, is counted as *one* "person" in the cume reach of the station. That same person showing a five-minute listening to a specific radio station during an additional 15-minute time period will then be counted as second "person." Therefore, a person who listens from the top of the hour to 10 past the hour will be counted as *one* person. The same person listening from 10 past the hour to 20 past the hour may be considered as one person in the cume from :00 to :15 and one person in the cume from :15 to :30 ... or a total of *two* people. Therefore it has been the effort of programmers for many years to locate spot clusters away from the quarter and half hour breaks and to attempt to sweep music across those breaks in order to encourage persons filling out ratings diaries to show themselves as having listened in more than one quarter of the broadcast hour. Thus the term "quarter hour maintenance."

As we discuss each of the hot clock example diagrams, placement of spot schedules to encourage quarter hour maintenance will be obvious. Also obvious will be the fact that as the commercial load increases, the attempt to keep the spot clusters away from the quarter hour break becomes increasingly difficult.

Hot Clock 1

Refer to Fig. 1. Note that we have decided for this discussion that our broadcast hour will contain two five-minute newscasts. Each newscast will carry one :60 spot and qualify for four minutes of logged news credit.

Our hour will carry ten minutes of commercial announcements, eight of which will be carried in four two-minute/three unit spot sets. The hour will then maximize at ten minutes/14 units.

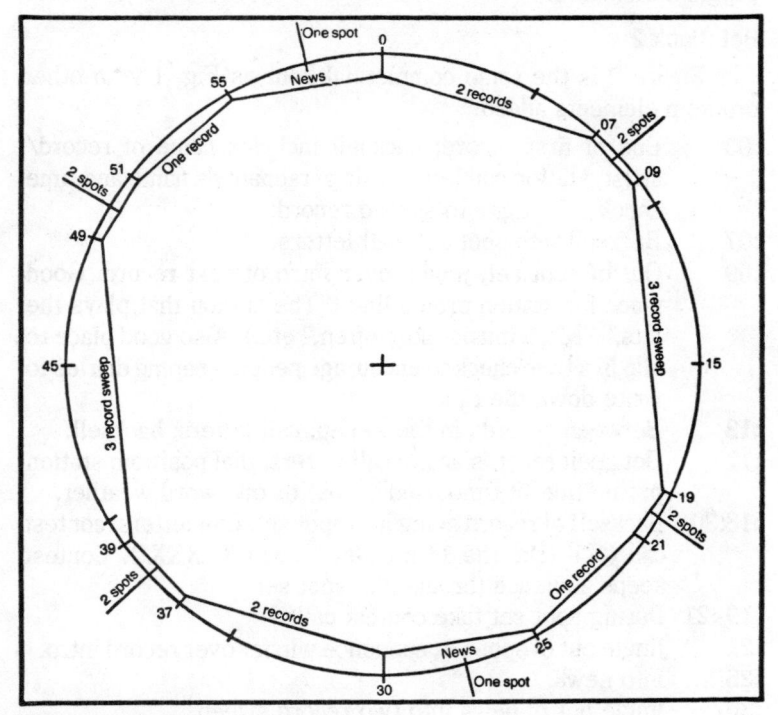

Fig. 1. Hot Clock 1.

Reviewing the hour:

:00-:07 Two record music sweep to introduce the hour coming out of the five minute news break at :55.
:07-:09 Two minutes/three units of commercials.
:09-:19 Three record music sweep across the quarter hour for listener maintenance.
:19-:21 Two minutes/three units of spots.
:21-:25 One record.
:25-:30 Five minutes of news, weather, sports, including one :60 spot.
:30-:37 Two record sweep out of news.
:37-:39 Two minutes/three units of spots.
:39-:49 Three record sweep across the quarter hour.
:49-:51 Two minutes/three units of spots.
:51-:53 One record.
:55-:00 Five minutes of news with one :60 spot.

Note that in Fig. 1 all we have accounted for is news and commercial announcements. No provision has been made for other program elements.

Hot Clock 2

Figure 2 is the same commercial hour as Fig. 1 with other program elements added.

:03 End of first record; backsell includes name of record/artist, station call letters, air personality's name and time check . . . segue to second record.
:07 Backsell into spot set; call letters.
:09 Out of spot set; jingle; over intro of next record. Good place for station promo line ("The station that plays the hits," "More music-more often," etc.). Also good place to slip in a time check to encourage people keeping diaries to write down the time.
:12 Between records in the sweep; call letters; backsell.
:17 Between records again; call letters; dial position; station promo line (if time used at :09) or one word weather.
:18:30 Backsell of record going into spot set. Call letters; contest call ("I'll take the 14th caller to win XXXXX"). Contest keeps audience through the spot set.
:19-:21 During spot set take contest calls.
:21 Jingle out of spot set; announce winner over record intro.
:25 Into news.
:30 Jingle out of news into two record sweep.

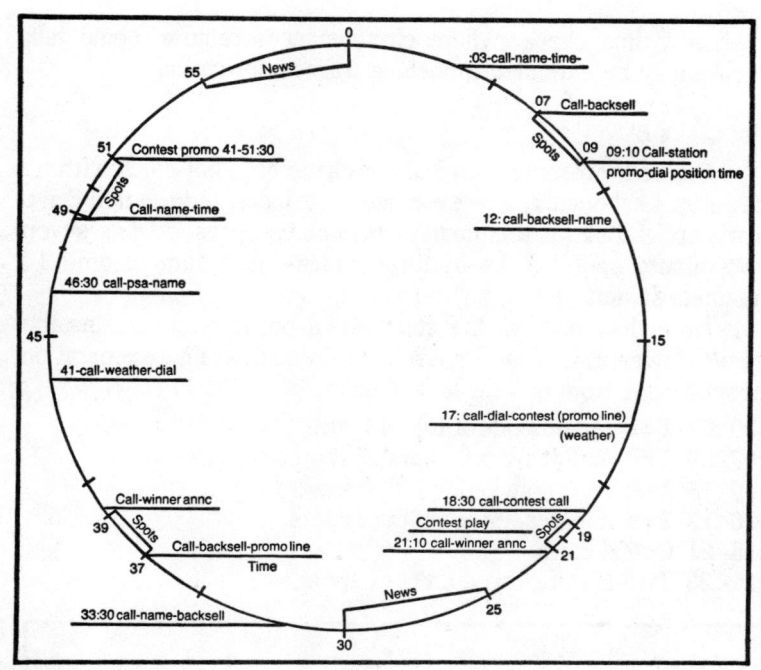

Fig. 2. Hot Clock 2.

:33:30   Call letters; your name; promo line. (Time check is never used in this position. Listing :33 in diary will eliminate five minute listening period for the quarter hour.)

:37   Going into spot set; call letters; backsell; promo line or time.

:39   Out of spot set; jingle; winner promo ("WXXX-Where John Jones just won a XXXX album from the Big 99—your chance to win coming up in minutes") over intro of record.

:42   Call letters; dial position; one line weather.

:46:30   Call letters; your name; PSA.

:49   Call letters; time check; backsell.

:51   Call letters; :30 contest promotion spot coming out of spot set; jingle into record.

:55   News; :60 spot.

:00   I.D.

Combining the information in Figures 1 and 2 presents a fairly complete broadcast hour.

In some circumstances more weather lines may need to be included in talk breaks. In morning drive, each talk break may contain a time check. Where circumstances require, some talk breaks may be extended to include traffic information.

Hot Clock 3

Figure 3 presents a typical non-drive hour hot clock with no newscasts scheduled. However, we have increased the non-drive commercial load for this hour to 14 minutes, presented as seven two-minute spot breaks of three units—maximum loading 14 minutes/21 units.

Note that much of the commercial positioning remains the same. However, it is now impossible to keep five minute separation of spot loads from quarter hour breaks.

:00-:07 Two records out of top of hour.
:07-:09 Two minutes/three units of spots.
:09-:16 Two record sweep.
:16-:18 Two minutes/three units of spots.
:18-:21 One record.
:21-:23 Two minute/three units of spots.

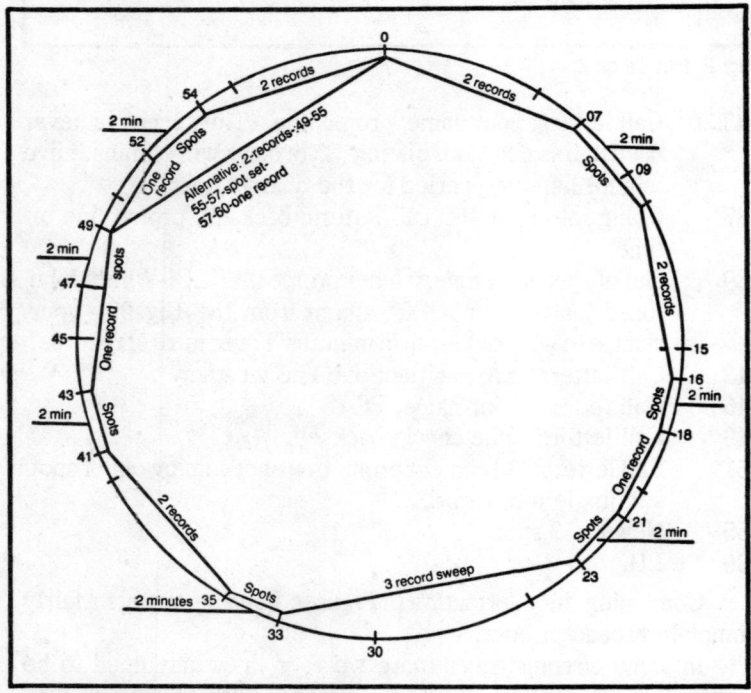

Fig. 3. Hot Clock 3.

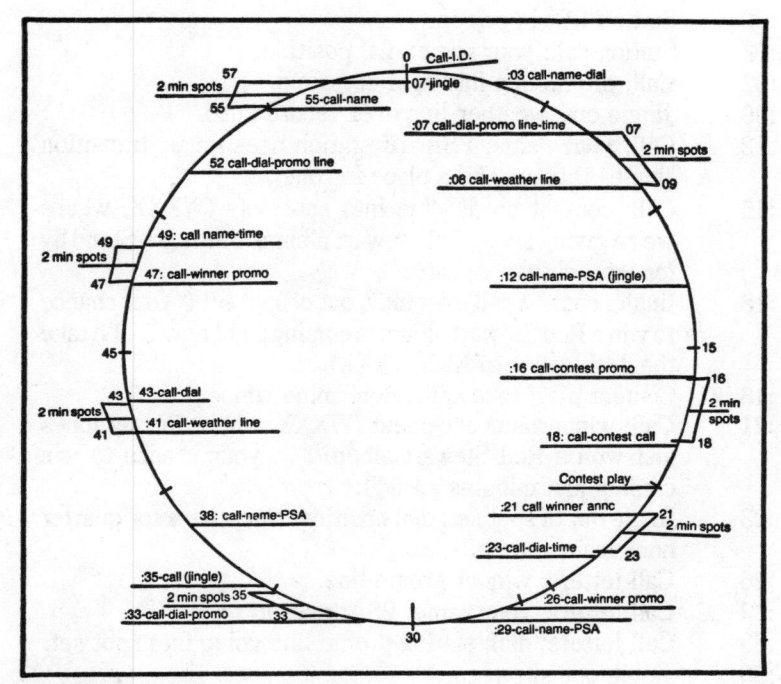

[Clock diagram with the following labels around the circle, starting at 0 and going clockwise:]

- 0 Call-I.D.
- :07-jingle
- :03 call-name-dial
- :07 call-dial-promo line-time
- 07 / 2 min spots / 09
- :08 call-weather line
- :12 call-name-PSA (jingle)
- :16 call-contest promo
- 15 / 2 min spots / 16
- 18: call-contest call / 18
- Contest play
- :21 call winner annc
- 21 / 2 min spots / 23
- :23-call-dial-time
- :26-call-winner promo
- :29-call-name-PSA
- 30
- :33-call-dial-promo
- 2 min spots 35 / 33
- :35-call (jingle)
- 38: call-name-PSA
- 45
- 43 / 2 min spots / 41
- 43-call-dial
- :41 call-weather line
- 49 / 2 min spots / 47
- 49: call name-time
- 47: call-winner promo
- 52 call-dial-promo line
- 55-call-name
- 57 / 2 min spots / 55

Fig. 4. Hot Clock 4.

:23-:33 Three record sweep.
(*Note*: PD may prefer a two record sweep from :18-24, spot load from :24-26, and another two record sweep to :33.)
:33-:35 Two minutes/three units of spots.
:34-:41 Two records.
:41-:43 Two minutes/three units of spots.
:43-:47 One record.
:47-:49 Two minutes/three units spots.
:49-:52 One record.
:52-:54 Two minutes/three units spots.
:54-:00 Two record sweep to top of hour
(*Option:* Note that this option gives a four record sweep across the top of the hour from :54 to :07. PD may prefer a two record sweep :49-:55, spot break from :55-:57, and a three record sweep across the top of the hour :57-:07.)

Hot Clock 4

Figure 4 shows the same hour as Fig. 3 with program elements added.

29

Time	Description
:00	Station I.D. in sweep.
:03	Station call; your name; dial position.
:07	Call; promo line into spot set; time.
:09	Jingle out; weather line over record intro.
:12	Call; your name; PSA. (If station uses music transition jingles this may be a place for one).
:16	Call; contest promo line into spot sets (WXXX, where we're giving away Rod Stewart albums this hour. Stand by for your chance to win).
:18	Jingle; contest call over intro out of spot set ("Your chance to win a Rod Stewart album is coming right now... I'll take the 14th caller to XXX-XXXX).
:18-:21	Contest play; take calls; determine winner.
:21	Call; winner announcement (WXXX, where Johnny Jones just won a Rod Stewart album... your chance to win coming just minutes away").
:23	Jingle out of spot set; dial position; time check for quarter hour maintenance.
:26	Call letters; winner promo line.
:29	Call letters; your name; PSA; over intro.
:33	Call letters; dial; station promo line going into spot set.
:35	Jingle out into record.
:38	Call letters; your name; PSA-time check on other business.
:41	Call letters; weather line going into spot set.
:43	Jingle out; dial position into record.
:47	Call letters; winner promo line into spots.
:49	Jingle out; your name; time check.
:52	Call letters; dial position; station promo line.
:55	Call letters; name into spot set.
:57	Jingle into record.
:00	I.D.

You will note that every break designed into the hot clock contains either a call letter mention or a jingle. One of the most significant factors in programming success is the ability of the audience to identify the station they are listening to. *Never take that fact for granted*. Design into the hot clock as many opportunities for station call letter mentions as possible.

When possible, the hot clock design should include as many dial position locations as feasible. Where a combination of call letter/dial position can be effected, such a combination has often proved to be successful. For example, Y-100 identifies the station (for ARB purposes) and identifies the dial position at the same time). Although such combinations of call letters and dial position are not generally considered a legal I.D., they do provide high identifiability for programming/ratings purposes.

Note also that time checks are usually scheduled at positions designed to aid in quarter hour maintenance procedures. Time is rarely given at :03 or :08, :17, :27, or any other position within the five minute framework from the quarter hour. Time is usually identified at a position designed to encourage listeners to take note of the time at a period such as to indicate five minutes of listening within the quarter hour.

Special notice should be given to the fact that it is illegal to give false notice of the exact time with the intent to deceive the listener into making note of the incorrect time for purposes of distorting listening times. Several years ago it was charged that certain stations made special note and emphasis on time checks featuring :10, :20, :40, and :50 minute designations, regardless of the exact time with an eye to deceiving the listener into indicating extended listening times in diary reports. (*Example:* Although the record may end at :18:30 and the segue into the spot set was to come at that time, the time on the air would be given as :20 past the hour. It was felt that should the correct time be noted at :18:30, and the listener changed stations at that point, showing a dial change time of :18 would eliminate that person as one who listened for a "5 minute period within the specific 15 minute period" of the rating and cause that person to be lost as a "person" in the cume/quarter hour body count.)

Each hot clock design, for each station, and each time period is a combination of necessary program elements and subjective evaluation of listener perception. The hot clock for each station may differ according to its needs.

The existence of the hot clock, however, is vital to the maintenance of continuity through each broadcast hour and provides the air personalities with a solid format on which to rely to ensure inclusion of all program elements in the hour. It also provides the program director with a format clock against which to evaluate the performance of each of his personnel and into which to design additional program elements as they are required.

Music Clocks

The second step in hot clock design is the programming into the hot clock of the music rotation. For purposes of this discussion

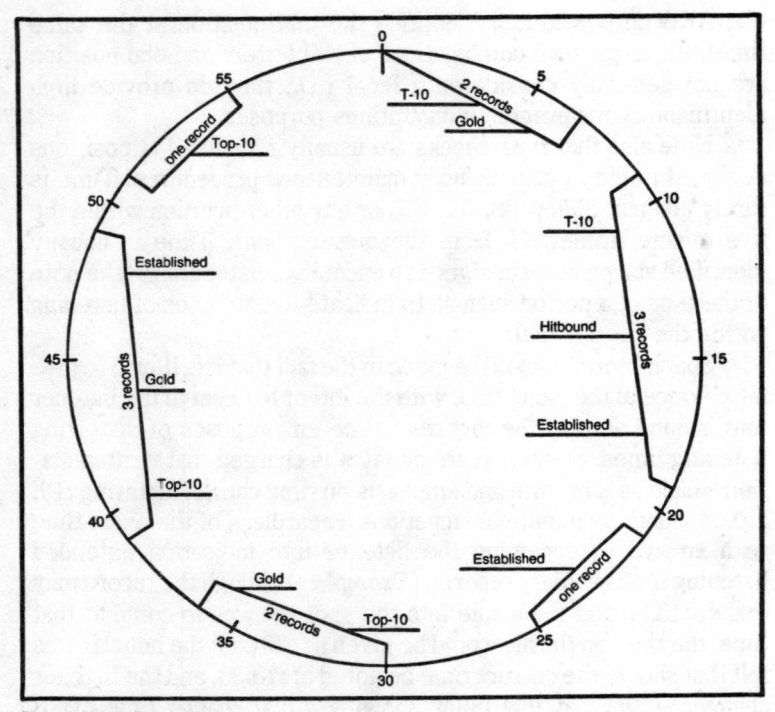

Fig. 5. Hot Clock 5.

we will use the same program hours shown in Figs. 1 and 3. Figure 5 indicates the music content identified in the hour shown in Fig. 1 and allows for 12 records to be programmed. Figure 6 shows the music content identified in the hour shown as Fig. 3 and allows for 14 records to be programmed.

According to the formula used to establish music content (described in the section titled "Formula For Computing The Number of Records You Should Play" in Chapter 4) we have determined that the music content of each of these hours should be as follows.

Figure 5 hour = 5 Top 10 records.
4 Goldens.
1 Hitbound.
2 Established Hits.

Figure 6 hour = 5 Top 10 Records.
4 Goldens.
1 Hitbound.
4 Established Hits.

Definitions

Top 10: Records indicated as Top 10 in popularity in our program area as determined by sales reports, phone research, and other verification methods.

Goldens: Past hits and recent Top 10 hits (recurrents) with demonstrated demographic appeal.

Hitbound: New records which initial research has indicated have Top 10 record potential.

Established Hits: The "bottom 20" of the Top 30, comprised of Top 10 records falling in popularity and Hitbounds building toward Top 10 status.

Given this music content we would probably program our music hot clock as follows:

Hot Clock 5

Figure 5 indicates six music sets divided as follows:

Set 1 — Two records.
Set 2 — Three records.
Set 3 — One record.
Set 4 — Two records.
Set 5 — Three records.
Set 6 — One record.
Total = Twelve records.

Set 1: Top of the hour, coming out of news. Program a strong record (Top 10 up-tempo), follow with strong Golden. Should music rotation provide slow tempo Top 10 record availability, switch order programming Golden up-tempo first.

Set 2: Out of stop set. Lead with Top 10 record, freshen music outlook with Hitbound, cushion impact of new music by surrounding HB with a solid Established Hit in the sweep.

Set 3: Single record, standing along between stop set and news. Play only Established Hit of mass appeal.

Set 4: Out of news. Top 10 hit followed by Golden; Interchange rotation if impact needed.

Set 5: Lead with Top 10, follow with Golden, close with Established Hit for a dynamite sweep.

Set 6: Standing along between stop set and news. Take no chances—hold audience with a Top 10 smash.

Hot Clock 6

Figure 6 indicates seven music sets divided as follows:

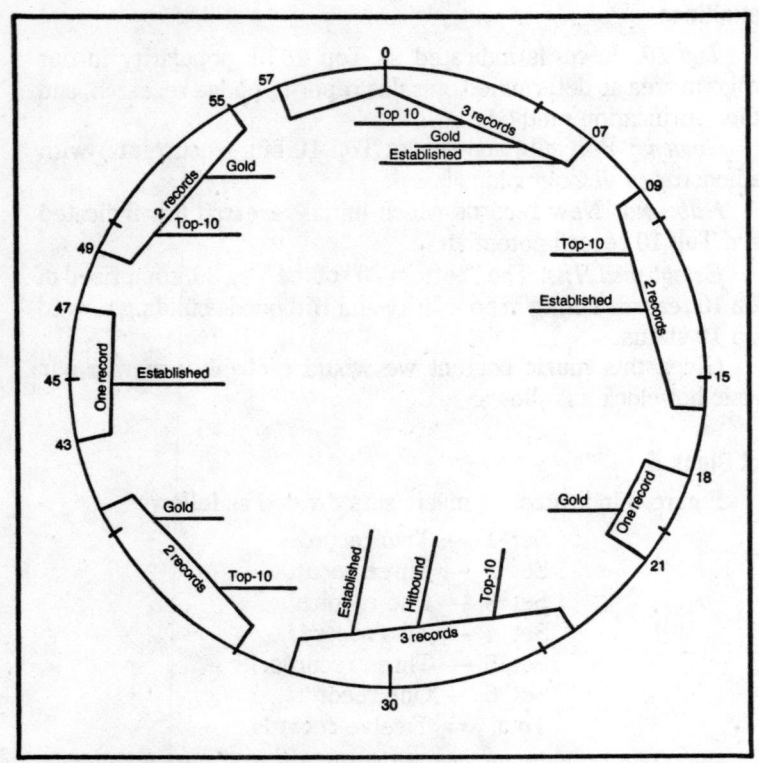

Fig. 6. Hot Clock 6.

- Set 1 — Three record sweep.
- Set 2 — Two records.
- Set 3 — One record.
- Set 4 — Three record sweep.
- Set 5 — Two records.
- Set 6 — One record.
- Set 7 = Two records.

Set 1: An extremely important set because it sweeps the top of the hour. Lead with Top 10 smash, follow with Golden, close with Established Hit. Keep tempos bright.

Set 2: Top 10 out of stop set followed by an Established Hit.

Set 3: Standing alone between two stop sets. Program maximum strength, mass appeal Golden.

Set 4: Top 10 lead, freshen music with Hitbound, cushion impact of new music with Established Hit.

Set 5: Top 10 followed by Golden.

Set 6: Another record standing alone. Program mass appeal Established Hit.

Set 7: Top 10 followed by Golden into stop set.

A study of the music clock examples shown will indicate the following:

☐ Reach for maximum impact out of stop sets and news breaks. This may be in terms of smash Top 10 records or established Golden hits. The object is to provide solid music values with which to recapture audience attention which may have wandered during talk/commercial segments.

☐ Golden records exist for much more than nostalgia value. The real value of programming Golden hits is that they have established, demonstrable demographic appeals. As we shall discuss further in the chapters on music, those demonstrable music appeals can be utilized as programming tools to attract specific audience composition.

☐ Whenever the transition must be made between stop sets or stop set and news without benefit of music sweeps, it requires the programming of solid mass appeal records, either Established Hits or Goldens, with proven values. This is the weakest time slot for programming Hitbound or other new material.

☐ When programming Hitbound or new material, it makes good program sense to cushion the impact of the unfamiliar music by programming solid, hit, recognizable music on either side of the "new" music. This technique provides minimum audience trauma and reduces possibility of tuneout.

As in the construction of hot clocks for commercial placement or program element location, the music hot clock provides the air personality with a solid foundation and reasoning for his music programming and a firm continuity to the program hours.

WHAT IS PERSONALITY?

I think the most misunderstood word in the programmer's lexicon is *personality.*

Assume that you are a program director asked to add "personality" to your programming. Where would you start? What would you do? What would you ask your air people to do?

In too many cases the word "personality" has been interpreted to mean "talk." Talk pieces are added to the air. Personalities are asked to be funny, to relate, to make topical comments. We've all heard these abortive attempts.

Personality stations are often viewed as different from "format" stations by slower pacing and less precise on-air production. To adopt either of these would be a gross error.

None of this goes to the heart of *personality*. Personality is simply the expression of the sum total of collective experience. The expression of your background, your emotions, your experiences, and your observations defines your personality.

Radio is no different. Personality on the radio is the expression, on the air, of your personality. Not everybody can do it. We've all met fabulous "personalities," people who radiate, people who can hold an audience spellbound. Many of these same people come across flat and lifeless on the radio. Their intangible quality we called "personality" may be a combination of audio and visual stimuli which are so integrated that they cannot be entertained separately.

Your personality is what makes you unique. It is the quality which defines you from others. We are all quite alike in a physical sense. It is the outward expression of our inner selves that people perceive and identify as our personality.

Some people are "closet" personalities. The inner self fails to adequately express itself outwardly. We talk about them as people "you have to get to know" to like.

Personality does not equal talk. Often it isn't what you say but how you say it that counts. Sometimes it's what you *don't* say that's important. The best example of this technique was the radio comedy of Jack Benny. Benny made the pause an essential element of his projected personality. It was what he *didn't* say that communicated his message.

Personality might mean warmth, humanity, and believability. The best radio practitioner of the "human" side of personality was Arthur Godfrey. His style, his laugh, and his comments made him sound human and believable. Godfrey sold soup for Lipton by kidding about how much chicken there *wasn't* in Lipton's Chicken Soup Mix. Audiences believe in Godfrey and they bought the soup, chicken or no chicken.

It's possible to deliver a ten-second line about the weather and sound human. Suppose you replace "Today's weather; sunny, cold, 35 degrees" with "Better wrap the kids up tight Mom, it's gonna be a cold 35 degrees today." It's the same information but you achieve personality. You will be perceived as caring about Mom and her child . . . all while delivering a weather line.

Personality demands concentration and preparation. Few great radio entertainers perform "off the cuff." Comedy, commentary, and interplay between air personalities and other people need to be planned. Write, edit, and rewrite. If it's questionable, get some feedback on it . . . or leave it out.

Jim King is a top-rated air personality who has worked WPOP-Hartford, WLEE-Richmond, 99X and WWDJ in the New York City metro, WNDE-Indianapolis, and both WHK and WGCL-Cleveland. Jim writes his bits out and never goes on the air unprepared. When we worked together in Richmond, Jim would write a bit, call me to test anything out that was questionable, rewrite, and then take it into the studio. *Every* top personality from Jim King to Ron Landry to Dr. Don Rose to Fred Winston prepares. Knowing you are prepared allows you to concentrate on delivery and style. Your *personality* comes through.

Personality means knowing when to be "on" and knowing when, and how, to get off. To a stage performer, getting on stage is easy. Performing is a little more difficult. Knowing when to get off is the hard part. Being able to time the point where you can "leave them wanting more" requires skill and timing. The radio personality who stays "on" too long can lose the audience. A radio personality who can't segue to the next piece of business—whether it's music, news, or a commercial—loses impact.

In the section on survey techniques I discuss a performer whose ratings dramatically improved when we put a ten-second limit on all of his talk. He was a classic case of staying "on" too long.

Personality in radio means never losing concern for the audience. Who are they? What do they want? What are their needs? *You* relating to *them* is what it's all about.

Personality means knowing yourself. Consistency is a major element of projecting personality. Inconsistency may mean you will be perceived as "erratic." This audience trauma is unfavorable. Knowing who you are and what kind of personality you want to project is most important. To a degree, it's like being an actor. You've created a character. On the radio you are that character.

Fill the audience's needs. For some it will be music, for some it's information, for some it may be companionship. Filling those needs is basic to communicating personality on the radio.

Chapter 3
Promotion

One of the old axioms of radio is that what you do on the air is only half the story. Telling people you did it is the other half. That second half is called *promotion*.

A great deal has been written about on-air promotions. No matter what you did on the air, the chances are that the only people who know it are your own listeners. You can't tell non-listeners what you did by using your own air. You've got to reach out and promote your station off the air to reach that audience.

As a participant and an observer of radio's outside promotions, I have seen hundreds of thousands of dollars in outside promotional activity wasted. The following review of outside promotional techniques is offered in that light.

OFF-AIR PROMOTION

Billboards are the most frequently used, and misused, outside promotion tool. Billboard use usually centers on two factors, design and placement.

With regard to design, to be effective, the board must tell the story at a glance. It is seen by drivers whose attention is concentrated on driving. The board is viewed as a momentary distraction. The most frequent design error is in placing too much information on the board to be absorbed at a glance. Simplicity in billboard design is the key. However, in making the board simple it is dangerous to leave out information by making unwarranted assumptions about the reader.

Case in point: A Los Angeles radio station board which indicated that X station (now shown by numbers rather than call) played "mellow rock." The first assumption the station made was that the reader was familiar with the change in the station's I.D. from letters to numbers. If the reader doesn't know that station KXYZ is now K-103, then a board which says "K-103 Mellow Rock" has no relevance to him. Second assumption: In indicating that K-103 played "mellow rock" the station wanted to tell the reader about a format change. They assumed the reader would pick up on this fact. It was pure assumption. The board did not indicate that it was a new format at all. Third assumption: The reader knows the difference between hard rock, mellow rock, and other kinds of rock. Aside from younger audiences, I do not believe the assumption can be substantiated. Fourth assumption: The reader knows the 103 in K-103 indicates the dial position of a radio station. My experience with other than young, active listeners indicates that this assumption cannot be relied upon.

Assume now that you are the billboard reader. You are driving down the road listening to your favorite radio station and you see the "K-103 Mellow Rock" billboard. Why would you change the dial to sample the station? Might you not assume that K-103 was a station you'd already rejected?

The board needed change (and was changed). The board needed to indicate that something "new" had happened, that a change had taken place. The board needed to ask the listener to do something, to take an action.

When dealing with billboard messages you *cannot assume* the reader knows who you are, what you do, why you are different, or what you want him to do. Your message must tell him.

The exception to this rule is the high-visibility station who may use billboards to reinforce call letter identification. In this case we don't want the reader to do anything more than remember the call letters. Therefore there is no attempt to ask the reader to take any action.

Placement is the second key element. Where are your billboards? Do you really know? Have you visited the locations and studied the physical location of the boards, the ethnic composition of the surrounding area and the economic conditions indicated in those areas? Have you plotted the board locations on a map of the area?

In one case when I bought billboards, I found that whole areas of our community could not be reached by billboards because of legislation preventing their construction. This made a considerable difference in the message we decided to use on those boards. You must know exactly where each board is, and who is most likely to see it. To recite figures on the billboard campaign's "reach" is not enough. Reach whom, and where?

Other questions need to be answered. Are the boards on the "going home" routes or the "going to work" routes? Major gasoline companies locate their stations on the "going home" side of the street because people going to work are too busy, too preoccupied, to buy gasoline. Doesn't it follow that people on their way home have more leisure with which to view your board?

In the case of double boards, which board has the higher readership, the inside board or the outside board? If the outside (or curbside) board has a higher readership, are you paying the same rate when your board is inside?

You must know the answers to these questions before making a buy in billboards. Don't be too surprised if the billboard salesman attempts to discourage your questions. He's selling billboards, not your radio station. He wants you to believe that all the boards he has to sell are good locations.

Bus cards: Questions to be answered when using bus cards include: Who are you trying to reach? Where do the buses go? Who rides the buses? When do the buses travel? Are you attempting to reach young people, old people, minorities, white collar workers, blue collar workers, citizens of the downtown area, or people in the suburbs?

Get from the bus company a map of the bus routes. Determine which areas of your community are served and which are not. You may find that in bus cards, like billboards, whole sections of your community are not served. This may make a difference in the message you carry.

Television is an expensive tool in most markets. Television is a "reach" rather than "frequency" medium. A great many people can be reached by each spot. It is not necessary to place a saturation schedule to reach your target audience.

Television has compiled detailed breakdowns of the audience composition of each program. It is possible to target demographically according to this information. If you know who you are trying to reach you can seek out specific spot locations to hit your target.

Assume that you want to reach a blue collar audience to bolster your 25-34 year-old audience. You may find that one spot placed in a program with high blue collar audience reaches as many people in the target as several spots run ROS.

Use the "reach" potential of television in placing spots. What is it you want to accomplish with your TV spot? Are you looking to "sell" the call letters? Are you asking people to sample the station? Are you seeking awareness of an on-air promotion?

Construct the spot to reach the demographic. A "great" spot that doesn't reach the target is not a great spot. If you are looking to sell adults on an adult-contemporary sound, perhaps the spot should concentrate on the "adult" rather than the "contemporary."

Most radio station TV spots do little more than reach the existing audience. A spot that features your station's sound reaches only those people interested in your kind of radio. I am familiar with a very successful TV spot campaign for an adult-contemporary station that played none of the station's music, features none of the station's personalities, and never asked viewers to listen. The campaign talked about the city in which the station was located and showed graphically how the station participated in, and was part of, the community. The station's 25-49 year-old numbers jumped markedly in the next ARB. We don't know whether these people ever listened to the station. We do feel that they wanted to be identified with a radio station that was closely identified with their community. They may have written the station's call letters in the diaries to gain that identification.

In television, what is perceived to be, *is*. The spot should be aimed at the perception level of the audience as opposed to the "reality" level. You have the opportunity to reach the "theater of the mind."

Other radio stations: Don't overlook this possibility. Although generally not available, it may be available in your community if you ask for it. I know of two examples where this technique was used. In the first case, a major top 40 AM bought the sign-off spot on the daytime black station. Since the station was signing off, their audience was displaced. It was told where it could go to find good radio.

In the second case a daytime black station was also involved. In this case the black station thought it preferable to direct its audience's attention to a white top-40 AM at sign-off rather than have their audience switch to a competing full-time black station, from which they might not return.

Daytimers, ethnic stations, religion stations and other limited appeal formats may sell you time . . . if you ask.

Newspapers can be advantageous but dangerous. For whatever benefit the newsaper can be to your station, you must remember that the newspaper is the major competing medium for advertising dollars. Any dependency placed upon newspapers to reach an audience may translate into increased credibility for the newspaper as competiton.

Here are some other considerations:

☐ Newspaper readership among young audiences continues to be low.
☐ Ads in newspapers are a one-shot proposition.
☐ Starch surveys indicate that newspaper "readership" figures vary widely from actual "awareness" by readers on a page-by-page comparison.
☐ Advertising rates are based on circulation. Circulation figures may have little relationship to readership and even less to awareness.

For illustration purposes, circulation may be compared to cume and readership to quarter-hour.

Newspapers do have considerable value. Purchase of newspaper ads may encourage reportage of your station's promotional activities. Newspaper ads may be used to reinforce on-air promotions and reach additional audience. Newspapers can be valuable in getting immediate circulation of entry coupons, music surveys, and other promotional items.

Newspapers can be a useful tool in support of station activity. However, you must not lose sight of the fact that you compete for the same advertisers. Every advertising dollar spent in print is a dollar not spent in broadcast.

Bumper stickers are generally used to raise call letter awareness or as part of an on-air promotion. They are limited by size, placement, and inherent nature as to message.

There is always a problem getting people to put bumper stickers on their cars. Prizes or a contest situation will most probably be required to get maximum distribution and display.

Weather presents a problem. Bumper sticker campaigns usually work best in good weather. Promotion is limited to summer in many parts of the country.

Litter boxes are a variation on bumper stickers. The station constructs a Kleenex-type litter box for display in the back window of the automobile. This feature makes the promotion playable in winter.

Milk carton sides are often used by country formatted stations. The station's message is presented on the side panel of home-delivered milk cartons. The message reaches the audience at the table. Cost, distribution, and logistical problems may limit use.

Mail stuffers can be effective. Inclusion of the station's promotional material in bank, utility or department store statement as stuffers reaches adult audiences.

Posters: Poster calendars have long life. They are most effective in reaching advertisers and prospective clients.

Book covers are a fine tie-in promotion with a sponsor for the fall. They reach a high school-aged audience, but logistics may be a problem. Some schools object to on-campus distribution of commercial materials. Design could be a problem; improper design may be perceived as "uncool." Remember, paper covers don't last. Plastic-coated paper is preferable but more costly.

Direct mail, although it requires production of a special mailing piece, has one distinct advantage. With the help of a mailing house, it can be Zip code pinpointed to reach Zip codes with weak ARB diary returns.

Outside appearances: There is no substitute for appearances by air personalities or station mascots in selling the concept of community involvement. Meeting the public on a one-to-one basis brings a "human" quality to your station. Clearly explained and written station policies on outside appearances will eliminate many potential problems. The charisma of your air personalities can be a potent weapon in establishing rapport between the station and the audience.

T-shirts, coffee cups and other items can be very helpful in obtaining display of call letters but this is generally an expensive method of promotion on a cost-per-thousand basis. Use of the promotional item may have no bearing on listenership.

Promotional items can be made more valuable by utilizing possessions to obtain discounts at sponsor locations or other perks. (For example, everyone wearing an X station T-shirt receives Y¢ off price of a burger at a sponsor location on a specific day.)

Telephones allow for two-way communication. The instrument allows the audience to reach you and you to reach them. Often used in connection with answering machines to take requests, offer information, solicit opinions or activate contests, the limiting factor with telephones is the lack of control over the demographic reached. Whether you call out or take an incoming call, you have little control over who will actually be on the other end of the line. Some problems with the telephone company may arise with regard to circuit overloads.

Failure to properly coordinate a telephone contest with the telephone company, resulting in overloaded circuits, preventing emergency calls from completion, could subject the station to serious penalties.

GENERAL RULES FOR OFF-AIR PROMOTIONS

- *Define the target.* Know who you want to reach and where the target is located.
- *Understand the limitations of the medium.* Every promotional vehicle has limitations. They may be reach, cost, or logistics. Understanding the limitations will avoid over expectations as to result.
- *Review often.* Even the best-planned operations fail. Never become so committed to a course of action or a promotional vehicle that you become inflexible.
- *If it isn't working, change it.* Changing a failing plan before it fails is maximizing economy.
- *Promote your promotion.* It isn't a promotion if nobody knows you did it. Doing a job is half the job. Telling people you did it is the other half.

Woodie Guthrie is reported to have said that "a writer doesn't write to write. He writes to be read." In radio we don't broadcast to broadcast, we broadcast to be heard. Promotion brings us the audience.

SOME ON-AIR PROMOTION IDEAS

Every program director has stories about promotions he's participated in. This section is not meant to be a catalogue of all of the promotions I've been associated with, nor even of the "great" promotions I'm familiar with; many of the great promotions are simply too expensive for the average station to do. What I would like to do is point out how some simple contest ideas can be used.

Jock in the Box: Perhaps the classic in radio promotion. In this promotion the player is asked to guess which one of the station jocks will jump out of the "box." The box actually consists of a cartridge containing, in scrambled rotation, the voices of each of the station air personalities congratulating the player if he/she picked him. If the player's guess matched the jock that jumped out of the box, the player wins.

This contest can be switched to a hundred varieties of play. On Valentine's Day the player guesses how many arrows cupid will shoot into a heart. On Thanksgiving, how many shots will the hunter need to shoot the turkey? On Washington's Birthday, how many chops will it take George to chop down the cherry tree? At Christmas, which of Santa's reindeer is hidden in the stable? The possibilities are endless.

Tom Shovan, when he was PD of WHVW-Hyde Park, N.Y., pushed the boundaries of good taste with Jock in the Box to new heights—or lows—when he played it this way: At the height of popularity of Loudon Wainwright's record "Dead Skunk in the Middle of the Road," Tom had his listeners guess how many "squishes" the skunk would make as the WHVW Prizemobile drove over it.

Boss Garage: This one was played by Dan Clayton as PD of WPOP-Hartford. A rotating cartridge was prepared containing the make and model of every automobile sold in the United States. Players were asked to guess, by make and model, the car that would drive out of the WPOP Boss Garage. The correct guess would win you the make and model car you chose. Possibilities ranged from Volkswagens to a Rolls Royce. (In preparing the cartridge it should be noted that some makes and models were entered more often than others. No attempt was made to make the audience believe that there was an equal chance for every make and model to appear.) In five weeks of play six cars were won. They ranged from an Austin America two-door to a top-of-the-line American car. Nobody won a Cadillac, Lincoln or the Rolls . . . but they *could* have.

Reaction was so spectacular that Clayton ran the contest again some months later. This time only one car was won in five weeks of play.

An interesting "switch" on the same promotion was done by Clayton following the success of Boss Garage. For weeks the audience was teased with comments that on March 1 WPOP was "Goin' Country." Country-accented announcers were imported (via tape) to say "Howdy, this is _____ telling you that on March 1 WPOP is Goin' Country." Only those with a need to know were given the details of the contest. Announcers and sales staff were told that there was no need to worry but were not given details. Sponsors were completely thrown. The station was besieged with telephone calls from listeners pleading with them to keep the rock format.

On March 1, Clayton launched his contest. In this Boss Garage switch the audience was asked to guess which country the WPOP jetliner was taking off for. They could win a trip to any country in the free world. If their guess matched the jetliner's announced destination, the player won the trip. As I remember, the station gave away several trips to England, one to Rome, and one to Japan.

Dan Clayton's "Goin' Country" was a masterful use of the switch in that it used a proven success formula in a new, exciting way.

After I became PD of WPOP I initiated another car-oriented contest. We called it:

Car-a-Day Giveaway: We gave away 31 cars in 31 days. To be truthful, I will admit that these were not new cars. They were used cars supplied by area used car dealers. If we had the budget I would have done it with new cars.

Cars were "hidden" all over the WPOP listening area. Sometimes they were on the street, sometimes in client parking lots. Clues were given on the air as to the make, model and location of the auto. For audience maintenance clues were spread throughout the day and recapped during the 4-7 afternoon drive. The first person who phoned us with the description and location won the car. They could have either physically located it or deduced it from the clues. This contest used elements of:

Treasure Hunt: The game is simple. Prizes are hidden and clues are given out on the air leading to the location. The audience is encouraged to find the prize. The first person to find it, wins it. *Warning:* Treasure hunts have, for the most part, been banned by the FCC. Some stations treasure hunt promotions have resulted in damage to public and private propery. Even though a disclaimer is run on the air indicating that nothing has to be dug up, turned over or taken apart to find the prize, overzealous contestants may damage property. There are ways around this: consult your station lawyer for ways to do treasure hunts legally.

Compassion Line: I believe this promotion is the brainchild of Pat Whitley. Pat did it at WWDC-Washington and WNBC-New York. I did it at WLEE-Richmond.

The station sets up a series of telephone answering machines tied to a special phone number. Listeners are encouraged to call the station's "Compassion Line." When the caller gets through a message is heard telling the female listener that, in spite of how busy she is, in spite of her daily responsibilities, when she thinks nobody cares about her, WLEE does.

When we did this promotion in Richmond, the phone company reports of calls completed and busy signals exceeded the total population of Richmond by hundreds of thousands of calls. The response was incredible.

This is a very cheap promotion to do. Check with the phone company before doing it. In any phone-oriented promotion it is possible to obtain a flow of calls which will overload circuits. Should this overload be responsible for failure of an emergency fire or ambulance call to be completed, the station could be held responsible. The telephone company may want to set up a special circuit for you.

Money Phone: A super idea. Players are solicited on the air. Player is told that the station's current "jackpot" is X dollars. Then money, in the form of quarters, dimes and nickels, is deposited into a pay phone. The player hears the sound of the money dropping. Player must then guess the new amount in the jackpot.

The advantage to this contest is that every player who loses perceives himself as losing by just a few cents. The non-player can play along at home trying to guess exactly how much money was put in the pay phone. Any player guessing the correct amount wins it all.

Second Chance Cash: A feature that can be adapted to almost any contest. In Second Chance Cash you give the losing player a second chance to win. Every losing player in your contest is told that "sometime within the next 30 days" the station will call again and give that person a second chance to win. Second Chance Cash is usually a much smaller amount than the original prize. The idea is to keep that player listening for 30 days. He's guaranteed a call. He just doesn't know when it will come.

The idea of "switching" the same contest has a beneficial audience effect. When you introduce a totally new contest, a great deal of air time is needed to explain the contest rules to orient the audience to play. If you utilize the same basic contest a number of times the audience has a point of reference. They know immediately what they have to do to play.

One of my favorite radio stations, WDRC-Hartford, Conn., has used endless varieties of "Jock in the Box" for years. It's one of the elements that give WDRC a very familiar and comfortable feel.

REMOTE BROADCASTS AS A PROMOTION TOOL

In the competitive, fractionalized arena of broadcasting, techniques need to be found to attract income. In situations where your station doesn't have the numbers or in smaller markets unserved by surveys or under the umbrella of larger markets, finding the competitive edge is increasingly difficult. In those situations, one technique which may be considered is the client remote—live broadcasting from a client location.

Before we discuss the advantages let's look at some of the problems.

☐ *Sound quality.* The station must have access to equalized telephone lines or clear channels on Marti broadcast equipment to maintain fidelity. Where unequalized lines cannot be obtained or Marti transmissions cleared, the remote should be scrapped. Salesmen must understand that maintenance of sound quality takes precedence over income. In FM stereo, sound quality problems may preclude use of this technique at all.

☐ *Logistics.* The physical problem of locating your air personality and broadcast board at a remote location can be difficult. If the physical appearance of the equipment is not impressive, the appearance may have a negative effect on the audience. Broadcast vans or trailers are best for remotes. Their size lends a physical presence which cannot be ignored and their insulation excludes extraneous noises from the air. If a broadcast van cannot be obtained, a collapsible booth can be built to surround the equipment and show off the call letters.

Now, the advantages of remotes:

☐ *Image.* The presence of your radio station at client locations, community events, and newsbreaks lends community image to the station. You show that you "care" enough to be there when something is happening. Conversely, the very fact that you are there, on the air, may make what is happening into an event. In smaller markets, "caring" may be your competitive edge.

☐ *Income.* When you are not selling numbers, you must sell "results." If, by your presence, you can get more people into the client's location and sell more goods, you can demonstrate results and build a case for the client to use your station.

Here are some things to remember:

☐ *Appearance.* Just as the presentation of the equipment must be designed to impress, so must the appearance of the air personality be designed to impress. Air personalities may be allowed to wear T-shirts and jeans inside the station, but on remote they should be expected to dress as though this was a "show biz" appearance.

☐ *Merchandise yourself.* Get there early enough to introduce yourself to the store manager and look over his products. Check unfamiliar pronunciations. During the news, check the progress

of the event. Show the client you care about this remote. This is an opportunity to sell yourself and the station to the client.
- ☐ *Merchandise the products.* If the client is providing "sale" items, you are in a position to offer your audience a bargain. Sell the product.
- ☐ *Perform.* Show yourself in the best light. Entertain.
- ☐ *Remember you are on the radio.* In a public situation, it's easy to forget that your main audience is still at home. Use the feedback from the radio at the location to inspire your *radio* performance.
- ☐ *Show the audience you love them.* You are there, you are available, you bring positive news about the client's promotion, you are human, you are real. Communicate l-o-v-e.
- ☐ *Stay legal.* Make yourself aware of regulations regarding logging and "substantial sponsor identification". Your station lawyer will fill you in on the guidelines.

When the going gets rough, creativity and ambition makes the difference in who wins and loses. Your willingness to take on the inconvenience of remote broadcasts may show your clients that you care about them. That may be the difference between winning their business and losing it. It's something to think about.

HOW TO GET GOOD PR FOR YOUR STATION

When Jack Thayer was President of the Nationwide Broadcasting stations, he embarked on a serious program of training for the general managers and program directors of those stations. An important part of that training was to develop the awareness of his people to the world outside the station.

As part of that program we were invited to Cleveland, Ohio one year to hear a number of speakers. Among them was the Radio and TV Editor of the *Cleveland Plain Dealer* newspaper, Mr. Raymond Hart. Mr. Hart shared with us his experience on how radio stations and newspapers could work together to their mutual benefit. Mr. Hart was kind enough to give me permission at that time to share his words and thoughts with others. Although Mr. Hart's comments were written several years ago, they are as pertinent today as they were then and bear repeating.

Getting good PR for your station depends upon a working relationship with the people at the newspaper, magazine, or other medium. The radio station must make an attempt to get to know the writer and the publication. This means digging to find out what the publication's policy on various subjects affecting the station will be.

Get all the facts and figures in your release. Be sure to be clear.

Explain what you mean. A release without an important fact or figure means that the writer has to stop writing and go digging for the information. That wastes time and delays his story. If you write something technical, add a P.S. to explain. Many times the P.S. provides more information than the story.

Compare the style of your release with the style of the publication. If you can learn to write in the style of the publication it makes life easier for everybody.

Use the telephone. Keep in contact. Call to say hello. Keep that working relationship.

Learn the publication's deadlines. Copy that comes in after a deadline misses publication or forces the writer to go in and ask for more space. It's awkward. Space is at a premium, but if the story is important enough, the publication will try to make space for it.

Don't get concerned with who needs who the most. It's a 50-50 deal. The publication needs good stories, and you need the promotion space.

Keep biographical sketches up to date. If one of your people does something, make sure you have an up-to-date bio on them.

Furnish the publication with up-to-date schedule information.

Keep an up-to-date history of the station. When something happens it's always good to reach back into the past to relate it to something else. It provides a fresh angle to an old story.

Keep pictures of your people on hand. Send copies to the paper.

When you call, if you can tip the publication to something that's happening at another station, do it. It expands their list of sources.

Learn the writer's idiosyncracies. We all have them. Know who you're dealing with.

Get to know the writers in various sections of the publication. Not all stories fit on the entertainment page. The sports writer or fashion writer may be able to give you space.

Be yourself, be honest, don't try to con the publication. Sooner or later you'll trip yourself up.

You like to feel important; so does the writer. Be professional.

In discussing policy at the *Cleveland Plain-Dealer*, Mr. Hart indicated that the newspaper does not promote radio promotional contests. If this is the case at the newspaper you deal with, get to know it. Newspapers compete with radio for advertising dollars. They are not overly anxious to promote their competition. However, newspapermen are in the business of news. Most professional newspapermen take that commitment seriously. If you have a story which is news, follow the guidelines and you'll see your call letters in print more often.

REGISTRATION OF WORDS, TRADEMARKS, AND IDENTIFYING SLOGANS

The registration of words, trademarks and identifying slogans by a radio station can be a useful competitive weapon.

Kevin Sweeney, the creator of a marvelous radio sales promotion called Bridal Fair and the former President of the RAB, tipped me to the fact that trademarks must be registered in every state of the union. There is no national registration of trademarks. Consequently, although he created Bridal Fair, Keven lost control of the name in Canada because he failed to register there and almost lost control in some states in the U.S. because he was slow in registering. Keeping that in mind I was able to use trademark registration as a competitive weapon.

Several years ago, Jack McCoy created a contest called the "Last Contest." I promptly created an entirely different contest and put it on the air with the title the "Last Contest." We couldn't afford to buy McCoy's Last Contest idea and we wanted to use the name so that my competitor couldn't buy McCoy's idea and use it.

I got a call from the Last Contest lawyers advising me that the Last Contest was a registered entity and that any attempt to duplicate the contest was illegal. I could, however, purchase the contest for my station if I wished.

Our reply indicated the following:

☐ The "Last Contest" on our station was in no way connected with, nor did it resemble in form or fact, the Last Contest idea being sold by their company.
☐ The words "Last Contest" were a registered trademark of *my* station in that state.
☐ Should they sell their Last Contest idea in my state it would be illegal for them to use that title since it was owned by my station.

Whether or not my attempt to register the Last Contest would have withstood legal challenge, I don't know. I do know that while the case was in litigation I could have prevented the use of the name by anybody else since we already had the name on the air. Whatever the circumstances, the problem went away and I never heard any more about it.

A similar move to thwart use of words, trademarks, and slogans was done brilliantly in Phoenix some years after my run-in with the Last Contest. A friend of mine got a job programming a station in Phoenix. The program director of his major competition in Phoenix would be an air personality who had worked for my friend a couple of years earlier in Las Vegas, at KENO radio. My friend was a well-known practitioner of a radio format then known as "Boss." Air personalities were known as "Boss Jocks;" weekends were called "Million Dollar" weekends and the format depended upon use of catch phrases to identify each element. The competing program director was thoroughly familiar with the format and the key words and slogans included in it.

As the story goes, the competing program director, upon hearing that my friend would be programming against him, registered all of the "Boss" format words as trademarks of his station. I understand that he even went so far as to register the word "weather" as a trademark of his station.

When my friend got to Phoenix he found it almost impossible to institute his format. All of the words used in the execution were unavailable to him. They belonged to his competition.

Obviously, registration of words like "weather" would not hold in court. However, it took six weeks to process the case through the courts. During that six week period the ARB came and went. Although my friend was eventually able to put his format on the air, it would be six more months before the next ARB. In the meantime, the competition had beaten him by using his own format words against him.

If you come up with format words, trademarks, or slogans which you feel are essential to execution of your programming, it might be a wise idea to register those marks *before* you put them on the air.

THINGS TO KEEP ON FILE

In order to be prepared to capitalize on PR opportunities there are several items that need to be kept on file.

Pictures

Air personalities: Whenever a press release about one of your air personalities is sent out, it should be accompanied by a picture. Publications are more prone to print stories with pictures than with straight copy.

Executives and sales people: Same as above. If one of your people is honored (as by a sales and marketing club) the story should be accompanied by a picture.

Promotions: Doing it is only half the story. Telling people you did it is the other half. Pictures help tell the story. They can also be used for dynamic ads showing the station's community involvement.

Remotes: Pictures of your station at a client remote may be helpful to the sales department in getting more business. They also fit well into the promo pieces you'll help prepare for the station's rep firm.

Studios, equipment, and building: Will come in handy for updating the station's bio file.

Written Material

Station biography: A file of notations made whenever something significant happens. New employees, staff changes, management changes, promotions, participation in civic events. Whenever something happens, write a short note about it and drop it into the file. If you get the opportunity to promote your station in the press, the whole history will be available to you.

People bios: When one of your people receives an honor, information on where he lives, what schools he attended, family, civic organizations he belongs to, etc., provide color for the story and help you get added space in publications.

Description of promotions: Every promotion the station does should be written up for the files. What did you do, how did it work, who qualifies to win? Questions which arise later with regard to contest participation and legality can be answered quickly if files are kept.

Winners' list: To eliminate questions that could arise with regard to misuse of prizes or IRS questions with regard to contest awards, it is wise to keep a file of contest winners' names and addresses. In the case of major prizes, it might be wise to illustrate this file with pictures as well.

Chapter 4
Music

Every radio station that programs music should have a definite, written music selection policy. This requirement is necessary to eliminate problems with the Federal Communications Commission with regard to plugola/payola.

A sample music selection policy is included here. It is meant only as a sample. Your music policy letter should be tailored to your station's needs.

A SAMPLE MUSIC SELECTION POLICY

Records are received by X station through the mails and by hand delivery from record company representatives and distributor promotion men. All records are received by the station music director.

X station subscribes to a number of music publications and "tip sheets" which are reviewed weekly to determine the national standing of the music as determined by these publications based on sales figures supplied them by record labels and their own independent surveys. Primary among these sources are such publications as *Billboard, Cashbox, Record world & radio & records* magazines, Kal Rudman's *Friday Morning Quarterback, The Gavin Report,* and *The Brenemen Report* tip sheets.

Local "one-stop" record outlets and major local stores are surveyed each week to determine the relationship between records listed on the national charts and local sales. Among the outlets surveyed are (*list by name*).

Request calls to the station are tabulated and considered in music selection.

A record may be added to the playlist based on the following:
- ☐ National chart listings.
- ☐ Confirmed adds on major radio stations across the country.
- ☐ Local record sales.
- ☐ Our decision that the music is compatible with the station's demographic goals.

Final decisions on which records are added to the playlist are made by the program director. Air personalities are not given a voice in those decisions. However, consideration is given to unsolicited suggestions from the air staff.

Order of play is preselected by the X station music rotation system. Variation is allowed only to suit immediate programming problems.

Plugola/payola affidavits are filed periodically by all applicable personnel.

FORMULA FOR COMPUTING THE NUMBER OF RECORDS YOU SHOULD PLAY

The debate on whether a pop radio station should play a long or short list of records continues. There are proponents of a short number of records, repeated often, and advocates of a longer list of records, played less often. Some feel that high rotation of the same records produces a negative audience effect.

How many records should be on your station? The answer lies in the answer to the question "What is it you want the music to accomplish?" When you can answer that question, you can compute the most favorable number of records for your station using a mathematical formula.

We start with some facts and some assumptions:

Fact: Each broadcast hour contains only 60 minutes.

Assumption: Of that 60 minutes at least five minutes is used to broadcast news.

Assumption: On our theoretical radio station, 14 minutes of each hour is devoted to commercials, weather, sports, traffic, public service and other talk.

In our situation we deduct five minutes for news and 14 minutes for business from a 60 minute hour, leaving 41 minutes available for music.

Assumption: Average length of a record is three minutes.

Compute: 41 divided by 3 = 13 records available in the hour. If you assume an average record length of four minutes you will have only 10 records available in the hour.

Assumption: We want the Top 10 records in popularity to be broadcast on the station every two hours.

Compute: Ten divided by two is five of the 13 records available in the hour must be Top 10 records.

Assumption: We want each quarter hour to contain at least one Golden.

Compute: One Golden per quarter hour = four of our 13 records.

We have now accounted for nine of the 13 records available in each broadcast hour.

Assumption: We want to program at least one new record per hour.

Compute: 13−9 = 4; 4−1 = 3. We now have three records left in the hour.

Assumption: If we want the Top 10 records to rotate every two hours, we may want the balance of the chart to rotate half as fast, or every four hours.

Compute: Three records available per hour on a four-hour rotation. This category can contain 12 records.

Assumption: We play one new (Hitbound) record per hour and we want the new music to come up about every six hours. This category can have six records in it.

Now let's add up what we have:

    10 records in Top 10.
    12 records in next category.
    <u> 6</u> records in Hitbound.
    28 record playlist is mandated in this situation.

An increase in the number of records played in these circumstances means that the category into which the records are placed will revolve at a rate slower than originally planned.

Why plan for a specific rotation? The amount of rotation the program director plans for is based on the computed average listening time to the station by target demographics. (This can be figured by utilizing the quarter hour and cume figures for each demo in each time period.) In a situation where average listening time to the station is short, the PD will plan for a high rotation to assure that each short span of listening contains a high percentage of hits. If the listening span is larger, the PD can adjust the formula to slow down the rotation and take advantage of the longer listening time.

Where listening time is uncontrolled by outside forces, shortening or lengthening the playlist to alter rotation may be used as a technique to influence listening span. Where listening time is controlled by outside forces such as start times for school or work as related to normal times for rising, maximum listening time is prescribed and no amount of adjustment will influence these listening spans. Obviously, if a man going to work starts at 8:00 a.m. no music or feature broadcast after 8:00 a.m. will be available to him and you can't make him listen past 8:00 a.m.

Music rotation is most often constructed to take advantage of known audience lifestyle patterns. With that information at hand, the number of records proper for your playlist can be computed.

BASIC MUSIC RESEARCH TECHNIQUES

As competitive pressures increase, programmers become more prone to seek methodology to reduce the risk of playing records which may prove an audience tuneout factor. This pressure has brought the need for more (and more accurate) information with regard to audience music preferences. Music research has become a major tool of the programmer.

There are a number of methods in use for determining audience music preference. We will discuss some of the most common of these.

Weekly Survey of Music Outlets

On the theory that audience music preferences can be observed in the audience's willingness to purchase records, we have surveyed music outlets to determine sales information. Record shops, one-stops, and distributors in the local area are surveyed to determine which records are selling and which are not.

Several weaknesses in this methodology become immediately apparent.

☐ Many music department clerks have no dedication to accuracy in their reports. Often the information given is based on incomplete information. Developing a personal rapport with the clerks in major stores sometimes helps but constant changes in store personnel make this a continuing problem.

☐ One-stops may give more favorable reports to those records

which were purchased from the manufacturer on a "deal." Often, quantities of some records are received free, or nearly so, and the profit potential of these records is greater than the profit potential of the records purchased for full price. The incentive is to encourage play of some records by reporting sales in excess of fact.
- [ ] Distributors represent specific manufacturers. Their reports will be prejudiced toward those lines.
- [ ] Even if the information received from each of these sources is without prejudice, it reflects only the musical preferences of that portion of the audience that wishes to purchase records.
- [ ] Many well-selling record albums have been found to reflect home listening and not music preference for radio listening. Music researcher Lee Abrams illustrates this point with a story he tells about some research he did into a heavy-selling album by the Mahavishnu Orchestra. Lee determined that these albums were being purchased mainly for home listening, often by musicians. They did not prefer to hear Mahavishnu on the radio.

Study of Music Trade Publications

Music trade papers contact radio stations and retail outlets all over the country to determine which records are being played and sold. This information is collated and printed in charts and graphs.

There are problems with using music trades as a source:
- [ ] Each trade has its own methodology for collection and collation of information. Information with regard to methodology is usually confidential. Wide variations are often present in the positioning of the same record on different charts.
- [ ] External pressures are often exerted to obtain chart listings and positions. Some trades may be employed in promotional activity by record companies. Others depend heavily on record company advertising for their survival. Others use record sales outlets as major sources for information.

In recognition of this fact, some record retail outlets have used their position to obtain quantities of "free" records in exchange for reports to the trade papers. Some trades obtain listings from radio stations. The information becomes inbred. For example, a major station reports a new record to the trades. Based on this report the trade paper moves the record up the chart. The same station may use the chart move to authenticate moving the record again on his playlist. He reports his move to the trades and the cycle repeats.

Call-in Requests

Stations may log all incoming request calls. Interviewers obtain information on the record requested, the age and sex of the caller. Information is then logged in diaries. Diaries may be kept for male-female teens, 18-24 year-olds and 25-34 year-olds. Examination of the diaries by age and sex will give the researcher some idea of music preference.

In theory, playback of the music requested by 18-24 year-old males should help maintain that demo in the daypart or help attract that demo to a daypart.

Major problems with this technique:

- [ ] It's time-consuming and expensive. Request calls often run into the thousands. It takes people to operate an in-call request research program.
- [ ] Collation and extraction of information is difficult from mass data. Access to a computer would be useful.
- [ ] The number of calls received does not indicate unduplicated callers. The same person may call in many times.
- [ ] It's subject to "hype" in the short run. Request calls for specific artists and records will flood the system as particular stars make local appearances or do TV specials. As the mass of information grows, these abberations should level out.
- [ ] You are dealing entirely with an "active" listener who calls the station. Such listeners may comprise a very small percentage of your listening audience. Some estimates have reported callers to be less than 10% of listeners.
- [ ] Information will be highly skewed by age group. As age goes up, the volume of callers decreases. Some form of "weighting" might be needed.
- [ ] Inbreeding. The audience most likely to call in is your existing audience. It may help maintain their listening but it won't help you find out about the audience you need to attract.
- [ ] Regeneration of known information. The music requested is usually the music most familiar to the audience. That music is the music you are already playing. New information with regard to the music you *should* be playing may not result.
- [ ] You don't know what the music choices of the "passive" (non-calling) listener are.

Outcall Research

In an effort to find out the music preferences of the passive listener, radio has developed the "outcall" research technique. There are a number of outcall techniques in use. In one case, calls are made at random to persons in the listening area. When a respondent is obtained, questions are asked about music, station, and artist preferences.

In another case, short segments of popular songs are played on the phone to the respondent to determine likes and dislikes or familiarity of certain songs. This information is collated, examined, and used in determining the station's music playlist.

Problems with the out-call method include:

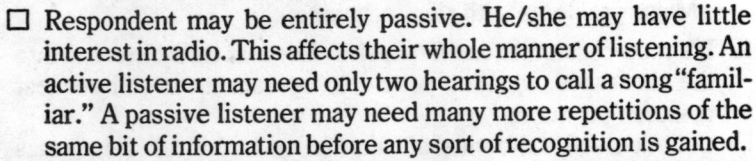

- Respondent may be entirely passive. He/she may have little interest in radio. This affects their whole manner of listening. An active listener may need only two hearings to call a song "familiar." A passive listener may need many more repetitions of the same bit of information before any sort of recognition is gained.
- A great deal of time and energy can be wasted obtaining responses from non-listeners. It's questionable as to whether their music opinions have much validity in relation to listeners.
- Information on new (or relatively unfamiliar) songs will be very difficult to obtain. If they haven't listened, they haven't heard it. As noted above, their perception may be different.
- Interviewer bias may be reflected in the interview. Interviewer may project his preferences to the respondent. It is not uncommon in such cases for the respondant to seek "approval" of the interviewer by responding as it is perceived the interviewer wishes the respondant to reply.

Outcall research enjoyed a flourish of popularity in the late 1970s. Unfortunately, many of those who attempted to practice this technique did so with little experience on how to analyze the incoming data. Many such practitioners failed to make outcall research a valuable part of their research technique. In the hands of experienced practitioners, outcall techniques can add substantial information to the programmer's pool of knowledge.

Some Conclusions

Observation of a large number of different kinds of radio stations utilizing many different survey techniques leads to a couple of conclusions. The first is that we have yet to define an infallible music research technique. Each technique has been subject to wide possibilities for error.

A second conclusion is drawn from observation. We have observed that a number of different radio stations have achieved success utilizing a wide variety of flawed music research techniques. Our conclusion is that there is something beyond research technique which is necessary to music programming.

The third conclusion is that it is not the information itself that is important. It's what you do with the information that counts.

Whatever the music research techniques, no matter how flawed the information, application of a consistent form of interpretation seems to compensate for much of the error. Changes in the interpretative procedures compound errors in the base information.

Some "formulas" which have been applied in interpretative technique are:

☐ Station requirement that a record must appear in a certain number of trade publications before consideration.
☐ Requirement that a record achieve specified levels of chart position in specified trades before consideration.
☐ Another method requires the record attain several trade paper "bullets" in succession before consideration.
☐ Another may require adds to stations with similar formats or in similar markets.
☐ Still another formula requires local sales action before consideration.

There is a theory that audiences seek musical identity as water seeks its own level. Under this theory, it doesn't matter what method is used for choosing music as long as the method is done with consistency. Theoretically, you could have your grandmother choose the music for your station. All those people with similar musical taste to your grandmother's would be attracted to the music on your station. If your grandmother has a universal ear there is every possibility that you could attract a mass audience to your station. As long as you don't change grandmothers you'll be all right. There have been some very successful radio stations whose program directors' or music directors' "ears" have been the major influence for adding music.

Whatever method you choose for music research, the more detailed your knowledge of your listeners and your community, the more likely you will be to define a method of interpretation which is to the best advantage of your station.

There is no substitute for knowing your market in music research.

MUSIC BUSINESS TERMINOLOGY

In dealing with the music director function of programming, the PD is often faced with terminology peculiar to the music business. We offer a familiarization with some of the most common of those terms.

Manufacturer: Refers to the record label, the company responsible for production of the record. In some cases the manufacturer actually manufactures the records. In most cases the manufacturer owns an office and the actual production of pressings, jackets and labels is done by outside contractors.

Distributor: A marketing channel set up to distribute a manufacturer's product over a specific geographical territory. There are two basic types of distributor. One is a distribution channel owned by the manufacturer as his own marketing device. A second is known as an independent or "indie" distributor. This distributor handles the products of a number of different, often competing, manufacturers.

The distributor's obligation to the manufacturer usually entails stocking, promotion, merchandising, and advertising of the manufacturer's product within the territory assigned.

The distributor system enables the manufacturer to have a specific number of accounts receivable, as the manufacturer will be dealing with a limited number (usually between 16 and 25) of distributors throughout the country.

One-stop: The one-stop is, in effect, a sub-distributor. The one-stop acts as a central stocking point for the products of all manufacturers. A retailer dealing direct with a distributor may only purchase the products the distributor handles. A retailer dealing with a one-stop has a total range of products available to him. This convenience shopping feature usually adds about 30% to the cost of the product over the distributor price.

Dealing direct with a distributor will usually require minimum quantity or dollar value purchases. The one-stop offers its customers the opportunity to purchase without such restriction.

Rack jobber: May operate leased departments in stores or stock product in racks in non-record retail locations such as department stores, drug stores, and convenience stores. The rack operations are often consignment deals in which the retailer pays only for the product actually sold as opposed to the quantity of product in the racks. Title to the property never passes to the retailer. Rack jobbing has become a major method of distribution for records in medium and small markets.

Because of limited space availability, rack operations are usually restricted in the amount of titles carried and are dependent upon high turnover merchandise.

The rack jobbing operations may be a subsidiary arm of a distributor. However, because of volume purchasing power, the rack may purchase directly from the manufacturer, obtaining prices competitive with the distributor's pricing.

Retailer: A term generally applied to retail outlets dealing exclusively or mainly with records and tapes. The term is not generally used to refer to rack operations.

Mom & Pop store: A term generally associated with small, local retail stores as opposed to chain operations.

Here are some examples of current record distribution systems:

W-E-A Distributors is a wholly owned subsidiary of the same conglomerate that owns Warner Brothers, Electra, Asylum, and Atlantic Records. W-E-A branches handle only the product of the parent company labels, their subsidiaries, and their distributed lines. Economies are obtained through central stocking and sales distribution.

Columbia Records owns its own distribution system, CBS Distributors, handling the products of Columbia, Epic, and Associated labels. Columbia owns its own pressing plants to produce products as well and for a while owned a chain of retail outlets.

Pickwick Records is a subsidiary of American Can Co. and is a fully integrated independent distribution, manufacturing and marketing company. Pickwick manufactures some of its own records under the "Quintessence" label. Most of this product is obtained as leased masters from other manufacturers.

Pickwick owns its own pressing facility pressing records for itself and other manufacturers.

Pickwick Distribution is a major distribution channel for several major labels, including at this writing Chrysalis and Arista Records. Pickwick maintains distribution offices in Los Angeles, San Francisco, St. Louis, Atlanta, Miami, and Honolulu at this time.

Pickwick rack operations have access to more than 2700 record rack locations within their distribution territories.

Pickwick retail operations include the Sam Goody stores in the New York area and the Music Land stores in the midwest. Pickwick's retail operations encompass something on the order of 430 locations.

Here are some other terms:

Returns: a term to indicate unsold merchandise being returned for credit.

Cutouts: deleted or overstock merchandise being sold by the manufacturer to recover pressing and jacket costs. This material is usually indicated by cut corners or record jackets or punching holes in the corners of same. Cutout merchandise is sold exclusive of royalty payments.

Schlock: Another term for cutout merchandise.

Promo copies: Royalty-free copies of records produced to be loaned to radio stations and other outlets for promotional purposes only. It is a violation of the Copyright act to sell promo copies.

Product: Industry term for records and tapes.

Free goods: Quantities of product given "free" to distributors, usual terms are one free or ten purchased (buy ten, pay for nine). Free goods may run as high as 30% on albums and 50% on singles in special situations.

Net pricing: The actual price of each record to the distributor without regard to free goods. Example: nine records at $3.50 and one free equals $31.50. For billing purposes, net pricing may indicate ten records at $3.15 each, or $31.50.

Master: The master finished tape of the music.

Mastering: The process of cutting the master tape into wax via a lathe using a heated stylus.

Dubs: Mastered wax copies (also known as lacquers).

Mothers: Positive image plates made from the lacquer to provide a casting mold for the stamper.

Stamper: A reverse image cast of the mother image used for stamping out the actual pressings.

Analog recording: Industry practice of recording music wave forms on tape to create the master.

Digital recording: In digital recording the wave form is not captured on the tape. The wave form is sampled 25,000 times per second and musical values are assigned to each one of these bits according to a binary coding system. In playback, the computer reads out the binary coding, reassigns the musical value, and recreates the musical wave cycle. What the listener actually hears is a broken wave. However, the rate of 25,000 times per second is so fast that it is not perceived as broken (much like the movement of still frames through a motion picture camera).

Digital recording is said to capture only the music wave without any of the distortion or variation induced by the tape.

At this writing, we have created the capability to record digitally but are still utilizing standard pressing and playback systems. Theoretically, the binary system can be imprinted in any configuration; we need not use present disk form. That coding can be read by laser and sent through the stereo reproduction system to eliminate the distortion or variations in sound quality presently induced by pressings, turntable, and stylus.

Chapter 5
Research and Surveys

There are three major measurement techniques used in radio for establishing audience levels and responses. They are telephone coincidental, interview, and diary.

In the field of audience measurement there were three major established companies. Each utilized one of the major techniques. They were Hooper (telephone coincidental), Pulse (interview), and ARB (Arbitron) (diary). For a number of reasons, the C.E. Hooper Company and Pulse firms have faded in influence. The diary method espoused by ARB dominates the field at the moment.

SURVEY TECHNIQUES

We will not discuss the merits of research companies. We will deal with the research techniques themselves. We will also discuss an exciting research company called E.R.A. (Entertainment Response Analysis) and take a look at what they may offer for the future of programming research.

Telephone Coincidental Surveys

Widely used for years by the C.E. Hooper Company, this was one of the early techniques. It maintains its validity under certain limited circumstances, as we shall see.

The basis of this technique is to assemble a group of telephone interviewers. Calls are then placed to randomly selected phones in the survey area. Questions are asked to qualify the respondent as to age, sex, and income bracket. Then the interviewer solicits information with regard to the respondent's preferences in radio listening.

Several situations become immediately apparent:

- ☐ The only persons who can be reached are those with listed phone numbers.
- ☐ Since the interviewer cannot see the respondent, qualification of the respondent is totally at the control of the interviewee. The interviewer has no way of knowing whether the respondent is black or white, young or old, wealthy or poor.
- ☐ The respondent's answers depend heavily on his/her ability to remember listening patterns. A "passive" listener may have difficulty in responding accurately.

There are several problems with telephone coincidental surveys:

- ☐ Under-reporting of ethnic minorities. Since it can be demonstrated that ethnic minorities have a lower phone ownership/population ratio, it is charged that such minorities are subject to under-reporting in a telephone coincidental survey.
- ☐ Persons with unlisted phones are eliminated from the survey. In some areas, this is claimed to represent a substantial proportion of affluent persons.
- ☐ Since the interviewer cannot physically see the respondent, it is possible for the interviewee to respond in a manner in which he/she wishes to be perceived, without regard to fact. Substantial discrepancies have been reported, particularly in the area of income evaluations. *Example:* The reader of comic books who is asked a question with regard to favorite reading material may indicate novels. The respondent believes that this response will cause him to be perceived as more "intelligent" than a reader of comic books. It has been charged that adult listenership is often distorted in the same manner. It is claimed that older and wealthier audiences tend to report listening to "prestige" stations, without regard to actual listening patterns.
- ☐ Dependence upon respondent's memory in terms of recalling a whole day's listening may lead to distortions.

The technique has proved useful in getting immediate measurement to specific programming features. It is widely used in television to determine audience levels "overnight." The respondent can be called at a specific time, while the program is on the air, and asked what program is being watched. These figures can be projected for the population and an acceptance level obtained. The same technique can be used in radio to determine reaction to specific weekend special programs or promotions.

Immediacy and low cost are inherent features of the telephone coincidental survey technique.

Interview Aided Recall Technique

Popularized in radio by Pulse, the interview technique requires use of a group of trained interviewers who are sent to randomly selected addresses to request information on listening patterns.

During the interview, the interviewer utilizes an aided-recall method. Should the respondent fail to remember which station or personality was listened to, the interviewer may aid recall by suggesting a list of call letters, personality names, and/or station sell lines to aid the respondent's memory.

Obvious problems:

- ☐ Obtaining and training interviewers.
- ☐ Logistics of interviews.
- ☐ Cost.
- ☐ The interviewing company must keep on hand a list of persons willing to do interviews. These must be persons trained to ask questions in a "neutral" manner so as not to influence the response.
- ☐ Because of work patterns and the need to catch people in their homes, the time available for interviews is short although each interview may take an hour or more to complete.
- ☐ If persons in the assigned home site are not available to be interviewed, the interviewer may choose another home on the same street. The randomness of the survey is often affected in this manner.
- ☐ It is charged that this method also tends to under-report minorities. Interviewers have found access to minority homes difficult. Language barriers and suspicions as to the real reason for the interviewer's questions are cited as reasons for this phenomenon. Some areas, identified as "dangerous," might be avoided entirely by the interviewing staff.
- ☐ It is also noted that many ethnic groups tend to "cluster." Any survey taken within that cluster may tend to be weighted by that presence. This has also tended to substantiate charges, in any interview survey of limited scope and duration, of "lack of randomness."

Advantages of the interviews method include:

☐ The interviewer is able to tell something about the respondent's background and economic circumstances during the interview.

☐ The interviewer can choose the respondent to assure the balance between age and sex in the interview is maintained.

☐ The length of the survey allows for more detailed and complex questioning. Sample dialogue might run as follows:
—What time did you arise?
—Was the radio on?
—Which station were you listening to?
—If you don't know offhand, was it X station, Y station or Z station?
—What did you do next?
—After you (showered) what did you do?
—What time did you go downstairs?
—Was the radio on downstairs?
—What station was it tuned to?
—If it wasn't tuned to the same station you had on upstairs, was it now tuned to station X, Y, or Z?
—After breakfast you left for work; what time was that?
—Did you drive?
—Was the radio on in the car?
—What station was on in the car?
—How long did it take you to drive to work?
—Did you listen to station X all the time you were driving to work?

The questioning continues until a complete listening profile for the day is completed.

☐ Because the interviewer can control the interview, gain impressions and information by observation, and because the interview is more complex, a higher degree of accuracy is claimed for the interview aided-recall method of audience survey.

Diary Method

The dairy is favored by ARB and in wide use today. The first procedure is the designation of the area to be surveyed, which may be Metro and TSA for a particular area. In some cases the survey area has been transferred to the television-oriented ADI. (TSA: Total Survey Area; ADI: Area of Dominant Influence.)

Homes in the survey area are provided with listener diaries in which respondents are asked to track their radio listening for a week-long period. Homes are called in advance to determine willingness to participate in the survey and the number of persons in the family unit who will participate. One diary is provided for each member of the family over 12 years of age.

The entire period to be surveyed may be as few as three or as many as twelve weeks. However, each diary-keeper keeps a diary for a period of one week. In effect, the survey period is a series of one-week diary segments covering the total survey period. A diary week usually runs Thursday to Wednesday.

Persons are asked to log their radio listening each day, noting each time the radio is turned on, to which station, at what time, when the station is changed, to which station it was changed, at what time, etc.

When the diaries are returned, clerks interpret the information with computers and the results determine the information which will be printed in the ARB books for the survey period.

Questions at the back of the diary qualify the subject as to age, sex, and income; Zip code designations qualify the respondent as to location. Names and addresses of respondents are confidential and not available to radio stations.

Here are some problems with diaries:

☐ My own examinations of diary returns for my stations over a ten year period show that most diaries are returned incomplete. The logistics of asking a person to carry a diary around for a week and indicate each time a radio station is changed prove too much. Most diaries are turned in with just a couple of days of listening indicated. These partial figures are projected by the computer to indicate total week listening.

☐ Diary return percentages according to demographic vary widely. Upper demographic returns usually outweigh population percentages. (Example: 49-64 women may be 8% of the population but diary returns from this group may be 15% of the survey). The crucial 18-24 demo usually returns diaries at a percentage far below their population percentage. (Example: 18-24 year olds may be 20% of the population but may return 5% of the diaries).

This discrepancy between diary return and population is accounted for by "weighting" the results. In weighting, the proportion of diaries returned is weighted to equal the proportion that demographic is in the population by increasing or decreasing the value of those diaries in relation to the total survey. Therefore, in the case cited, the choices of the 5% of the 18-24 year-olds returned would be weighted *up* to reflect the listening patterns of 20% of the survey. The 15% diary returns from the upper demo would be weighted *down* to equal 8% of the population. In cases where the percentage of diary return is low in a demographic, the standard deviation for error in the weighting is extraordinary.

☐ In some cases I have witnessed, diary returns for the whole family may show that the diaries were filled out by the same person. Unless listening patterns for each diary duplicate exactly, those diaries are not discounted from the survey. Case in point: Three diaries returned from the same Zip code; ages for male, female, and teen indicate a high probability that they could be father, mother, and daughter. All three diaries were filled out in red pencil and all in obviously the same handwriting. In this case, the survey would *indicate* listening patterns for three different demographics but would actually *reflect* the choices of only one of the group.

☐ Circumstances also indicate that when family groups listen together, as at breakfast, all the diaries show the same listening pattern. While this would actually reflect the *listening* of the group, it would not necessarily indicate the *preference* of members of the group.

☐ Another possibility for error occurs when transposition is made from the diary returns to the computer entry. In the case of AM and FM with the same call letters, the possibility of error exists if the respondent does not clearly indicate which station was actually listened to. In the case where transcription errors of letters within and among call letters occurs, one of the stations may receive credit or the book may be discounted entirely and both stations will lose credit. In cases where station "sell" slogans are indicated in place of call letters, the station will lose credit if all possibility of sell line combinations was not indicated to ARB in advance.

Although the possibility for error exists in all three methods, the diary return method seems to be favored as the best combination of accuracy and cost.

Although considerable possibility for error exists, much of the negative effect of such error can be overcome by diligence. It is further felt that when the results of a series of surveys is plotted, the incidence of error tends to cancel out and the plotted results indicate a "trending" pattern which is substantially accurate.

Entertainment Response Analysis

A unique form of programming research utilizing specialized

techniques, E.R.A. is the name of a consultation-research firm headed by psychologist Tom Turricci and programmer Sebastian Stone. The research involves the use of four techniques: galvanic skin response, operant perference testing, semantic differential, and confrontation.

A team of interviewers select, from the population in the radio station survey area, a sample of 40 persons who represent the age, sex, ethnic, and income strata of the community. Mr. Turricci indicates that a stratified sample of 40 has been found to be an ideal working number. Increasing the sample size increases the amount of data obtained without adding substantial information to the result.

Present technique allows for the comparison of four radio stations in a market. The client station chooses three with which it wishes to be compared. These may be direct competitors in similar formats or stations in other formats which the client station wishes to examine.

Simultaneous segments are recorded from the four stations to be tested. Segments are taken from morning, midday, afternoon, and 7-midnight day parts.

The stratified sample is exposed to the stations in the test group during the daypart in which the samples were taken. Morning segments are heard by the test group during the 6-10 a.m. daypart; midday segments are listened to between 10 a.m. and 3 p.m.; afternoon segments from 3-7 p.m., and 7-midnight segments are heard during that time slot.

Galvanic Skin Response: The test group is wired to galvanic skin response meters. These are similar to "lie detectors" in that they sample reactions to blood pressure within the person being tested. Each segment of radio is then aired for the respondent through headphones. Reactions to what is heard can then be plotted on graphs according to age, sex, and ethnic and income variations. (It should be noted that, other than extremely advanced students of yoga, it is doubtful that any of us can control skin response in reaction to stimuli. These responses therefore are entirely spontaneous.)

Graphs indicate response. They do not indicate positive or negative. It is necessary to interpret from further tests the *quality* of the response measured.

Respondents are told that their reponses are anonymous. They are unaware that researchers can define their results in terms of demographic breakouts.

Operant Preference: The test group is given a control allowing choices to be made among the four stations available in their headsets. The researcher has the capability of determining the position of the switches and when changes are made. It is possible to graphically plot the listening patterns of each of the groups when they believe their listening is anonymous.

Semantic Differential: The test group is given a group of words with 1-10 scales. They are asked to make judgments with regard to their listening. (*Example:* Rate a disk jockey on a scale of 1-10 from "lousy" to "great".) Further on down the test, the question may be asked in reverse, or with synonyms. Results are then compared. The object is to determine the test group"s capability to verbalize reactions.

Confrontation: The test group is broken into smaller groups and a discussion is held. The discussion is secretly recorded. Questions are asked which will stimulate discussion. The intention is to allow the test group to express their opinion and feelings on the radio they have just listened to.

What kind of programming information can be obtained? When I did an E.R.A. study at WLEE (Richmond, Virginia) in 1973, some of the results obtained were as follows:

Strong response was shown to a new set of jingles recently put on the air. Later examination showed the jingles to have caused significant reaction in the galvanic skin response testing. No one at any time during the balance of the testing expressed an opinion with regard to the jingles. We determined that the responses obtained to this set of jingles was negative and we removed them from the air.

Strong response to one of the announcers was noted from women. However, testing indicated that the response faded within a short period of time. We determined that this personality had a voice quality which was pleasing to women but that the content of his conversation was not holding interest. We put a ten second talk limit on all of his conversations and his ratings among women in the next book improved significantly.

Younger audiences were presumed to have a negative attitude toward commercials. However, very positive response to some commercials was noted. We determined that it was not commercials which turned young audiences off, but commercials of irrelevant content that alienated them. Working with our sales department, we developed a system of demographically scheduling commercial content. This policy diminished the negative audience effect of a heavy commercial schedule and assured clients of better acceptance of their message.

Universal response was noted to specific kinds of news information. Newscasts were restructured around these positive features to give the newscasts more power and relevance.

Some opinions with regard to age and ethnic perception and preferences for music choices were noted. When segments of the test group believed themselves to be anonymous, their choices of music varied widely from choices made when they believed themselves under observation. Conversation recorded during the confrontation section aided in restructuring the station sound.

Did it work? Information gained from this study was helpful in reversing the station's downward rating slide immediately. Eventually we reversed our rating position and almost doubled the stations income within a three-year period.

We did note a couple of problems, however. Any study provides a mass of data. Interpretation of this data is a key to its use. Also, the study is expensive. Time, equipment, the paid test group, interviewers, and hotel costs are substantial.

Conclusions

Research, whether done for audience measurement or audience preference, depends on the creation of established methodologies. These methodologies add standards against which to measure results. Each method has wide latitude for human and mechanical errors. Survey results are best examined in the light of results obtained from a number of surveys and plotted to suggest trends.

Research is a tool for better programming. Audience measurement provides benchmarks against which to measure success or failure of programming policies. To assign value in excess of this research, or audience measurement, is to distort the information obtained through the research technique.

UNDERSTANDING ARB

Currently, the most utilized technique for rating radio audience levels is provided by Arbitron of Laurel, Maryland. The company, known industry-wide as ARB, has created some new terminology and formulas which must be understood before the information in the ARB diary report can be digested.

To aid understanding of ratings, Arbitron (ARB) has prepared several booklets the serious student of rating techniques would be wise to study. They are *Understanding and Using Radio Audience Estimates: a Quick Reference Quide,* and *Research Guidelines for*

Programming Decision Makers: a Programmer's Guide to the Dynamics of Radio. Both books are available from Arbitron, The Arbitron Building, Laurel, Maryland.

Rating and Share

What we will provide here is a short explanation of some of the common terms and formulas found in normal discussion about ratings. The first three definitions we will concern ourselves with are *Persons Using Radio, Rating,* and *Share.*

To begin to determine these estimates, we need to obtain the population figure for the area we are to discuss. ARB will usually supply population figures based on population in the Metro Survey Area or the television ADI.

Given knowledge of the population figure, ARB will then extract from its raw data a figure indicating the number of persons in that population who were listening to any individual station in the survey and the number of persons who were listening to all stations in the survey.

Persons Using Radio will then be computed from the number of people listening to all radio in the survey expressed as a percent of the total population. If the population of the metro (or ADI) were 100,000 persons and the survey indicated that 40,000 of those were listening to radio, Persons Using Radio would be computed as:

$$\frac{40,000}{100,000} = 40\%$$

Rating for each individual station is constructed in the same way. Assuming the same population base (100,000 persons), the survey might determine that 15,000 of those people were listening to station A. Station A's rating would be determined as:

$$\frac{15,000}{100,000} = \text{a rating of } 15\%$$

We have now determined in our universe of 100,000 the percentage of persons listening to radio and the percentage of persons who were listening to station A. What we have not determined is how well station A is doing against the other radio in the market competing for the audience. That computation is called *Share.*

In our sample there are 100,000 persons in the survey, 40,000 of whom are listening to radio. Station A has 15,000 of those 100,000 persons listening to it. Therefore, station A's share of the audience is computed as follows:

$$\frac{15,000}{40,000} = 37\frac{1}{2}\%$$

Comparison of station shares will indicate how well station A is doing against other stations in the market.

To this point we have been dealing with total audience numbers and total survey population figures. While these figures provide some information with regard to rating and market share of the station as a whole, they do not provide information with regard to individual daypart or to age/sex demographic breakouts. We must, therefore, refine the figures further. The ARB diary report provides additional information for this use in terms of:

☐ Population breakouts by age/sex demographics for the survey area.
☐ Population breakouts by age/sex demographics for listeners to radio in individual dayparts.
☐ Average person audience estimates by age/sex demographics by station.

Average Persons is the estimated number of persons listening to a station during any quarter hour in any specific daypart. For example, given an Average Person audience estimate of 500 for station Z in the weekday morning drive 6-10 a.m. time period we would assume an audience of 500 persons to be available for each quarter hour segment of that time period, whether it is 6:15-6:30 a.m. or 9:00-9:15 a.m.)

Given the Average Persons figures by age/sex/daypart and the population breakout for the survey area by age/sex/daypart, we can compute the station's *Average Ratings* for any age/sex demo by daypart.

Average Rating is a percentage expression of Average Persons as a part of the population in the same age/sex/daypart. Compute by dividing the number of average Persons in a specific age/sex/daypart by the Metro population figure for the same age/sex/daypart. If our station had 500 18-24 males Average Persons in the 6-10 a.m. weekday daypart and the survey area contained 5000 18-24 year-old males in the same daypart, our station's Average Rating for Mon.-Fri. 6-10 a.m. 18-24 year-old males would be expressed as:

$$\frac{500}{5000} = 10\%$$

Average rating is always indicated as a percent.

Given age/sex/daypart demo information for our station and age/sex/daypart information for each daypart of the survey population, we are in a position to compute our station's share of the available audience listening to radio.

ARB calls this information *Metro Share,* an expression of the percentage an individual station has in a daypart of the age/sex demo in that daypart which is listening to radio. To compute Metro Share, divide the Average Person age/sex/daypart information for a station by the age/sex/daypart information provided for radio listeners. For example, we have determined that our station has 500 18-24 year-old males listening in the 6-10 a.m. Mon.-Fri. daypart and that there are 5000 18-24 year-old males in the survey area population during that same daypart. However, of those 5000 18-24 year-old males, it might be determined that only 3000 are listening to radio. Therefore, our station's Metro Share of the audience might be indicated as:

$$\frac{500}{3000} = 16.6\% \text{ share}$$

We have seen two examples of computation of rating and of share. In the first, we described the radio station in terms of total audience numbers of listeners against population. In the second we described average audience numbers by age/sex/daypart against survey population figures in the same categories.

In each case, the figures have been given as percent of audience. This sometimes leads to confusion between the terms *rating* and *share.* To clarify ARB indicates that rating always is expressed as a percentage of total population while share is a measurement against listening activity taking place.

The area is further confused when Average Person, Average Rating, or Metro Share figures are combined in an effort to describe the marketplace. ARB has stringent qualifications as to how such figures can be combined and how they cannot be combined. Before attempting any combination of Average Person, Average Rating, or Metro Share figures, consult with an ARB representative or obtain specific information on the allowable methods for adding or combining figures from ARB.

CUME

Many radio stations and programmers prefer to present their station in terms of *cumulative audience reach* as opposed to dealing in quarter-hour rating or share figures. This is especially true among contemporary music programmers who tend to feel that their stations have a high tune in/tune out factor, due to persons listening in for some music and tuning out for other program elements. These programmers are often said to be dealing in "body count" figures. The ARB survey report provides cumulative audience estimates in the form of Cume Persons and Cume Rating.

Cume Persons: is often compared to newspaper or magazine circulation figures. Cume Persons attempts to estimate the number of different persons who listened to *any* daypart week without concern for the length of time the person listened. Persons who listened for five minutes are counted as one person; persons who may have listened for the entire week are counted as one person.

Cume Rating: is an expression of the Cume Persons report as a percent of the total survey audience. In our example, our station had an Average Persons report of 500 18-24 year-old males in the Mon.-Fri. 6-10 a.m. daypart. We learned that this was 10% of the 18-24 year-old males in the survey area and 16.6% of the 18-24 year-old male listeners in that daypart. We may now determine that our station shows a Cume Persons figure for 18-24 year-old males, Mon.-Fri. 6-10 a.m., of 1500. Although 500 persons in this demo are listening in any specific quarter hour of our Mon.-Fri. 6-10 a.m., our station reached 1500 different 18-24 year-old males during that period. Computing is as follows:

$$\frac{1500}{5000} = 30\%$$

What this figure tells us is that while our station reaches 10% of the 18-24 year-old males in our market during *any individual* 6-10 a.m. quarter hour, we have the capability of reaching 30% of the market during the broadcast-week. This figure is often referred to as *penetration*.

Another figure provided for use by ARB is that of *Exclusive Cume Persons*. In this figure ARB attempts to estimate the number of different persons who listened *only* to your station, and no other, during the time period. This figure is most useful in establishing evidence of station loyalty.

As with Average Persons, Average Ratings, and Metro Share

figures, there are ways of combining Cume Persons and Cume Rating figures which are acceptable and ways which are not acceptable. Again, contact ARB with regard to specifics.

Maintenance and Turnover

Looking back on what we've discussed so far, we see that we know how many people are listening to our station by age/sex/daypart and we know how these figures relate with regard to our total market and to the number of listeners within the total market.

One of the things we might discover in examining those figures is that our station has a quarter hour figure which is significantly different from our cume figure for the same age/sex/daypart. (In our example we talked about 500 18-24 year-old men in the quarter hour and 1500 18-24 year-old men in the cume.) What we know from this is that three times as many men in that demo listen to us for a period of five minutes or more during the Mon.-Fri. 6-10 a.m. period than listen to us during any individual quarter hour segment in that daypart. We also know that there are 3000 18-24 year-old men who are listening to radio during that daypart during any specific quarter hour and we can determine from the report the number of Cume Persons available to all the stations in the market during that daypart. We know, therefore, that we have an opportunity and a possibility for audience growth during this daypart. Within our own station audience alone if we could get some of those 1500 Cume Persons who listened at *some* time during the week to stay with us longer, we might be able to convert them to increase our quarter hour listenership. Programmers often refer to this as audience *maintenance.*

Some of the techniques for increasing audience listening time might be billboarding of upcoming events to cause the audience to stay tuned. (Examples: "Coming up next the new record by the Bee Gees;" "We'll be back after the news with the number one record in the country;" "There's been a double murder in Gotham and we'll have all the details for you in the news, coming up in five minutes.") Or we could alter the music rotation (increasing rotation of hits to capitalize on fast audience turnover; slowing down rotation to lessen "irritant" factor of high rotation), or position features at such times as to encourage listeners to stay tuned for them. This could be anything from weather to traffic to ski reports to playing one Beatles record an hour all day long.

The common factor in all of this, however, must be some knowledge of what is happening today on your station with regard to length of time the audience listens. The amount of time spent listening can be computed by the use of a simple formula.

Time Spent Listening: The formula for this computation is as follows: Number of quarter hours in a time period multiplied by the Average Person Audience equals Gross Quarter Hours of Listening, divided by the Cume Persons audience equals Time Spent Listening.

To determine the first figure in the equation, multiply the number of hours in the daypart by the amount of hours in the daypart by the number of quarters in one hour (four) by the number of days in the period. For example the number of quarter hours in the time period Mon.-Fri. 6-10 a.m. is 80. For the 10 a.m.-3 p.m. Mon.-Fri. period the computation would be done the same way—five hours × four quarters × five days = 100 quarter hours in the time period.

Reverting back to our previous example, let's compute the Time Spent Listening. We were dealing with Mon.-Fri. 6-10 a.m., so our number of quarter hours in the time period would be 80. We said that our Average Persons audience for males 18-24 was 500. Using the formula, we compute the gross quarter hours of listening for this demo in that daypart on our station to be (80 × 500) 40,000.

We stated, in our example, that the Cume Persons report for our station in that demo/daypart was 1500. Continuing with our formula, we divide the gross quarter hours of listening (40,000) by the Cume Persons (1500) and determine a Time Spent Listening figure of 26.6 quarter hours or 6.65 hours (quarter hours divided by four).

By making comparison examinations of Time Spent Listening between your station and competing stations in your market, you'll get an idea of not only how many people you have listening, but *how long* you're holding the audience. If your techniques for audience maintenance work, you may see an increase in the amount of Time Spent Listening.

Another measure of how well you are holding the audience might be obtained by computing audience turnover. *Turnover* is simply how many times the audience changes during a time period. It is calculated by dividing Cume Persons by Average Persons. In our example, the Cume Persons of 1500 is divided by the Average Persons of 500 to show an audience turnover factor of three.

Under certain sets of circumstances, Time Spent Listening and audience turnover may be affected by circumstances outside the boundaries and control of the radio station. Let's assume a situation in a suburban community where the work force is dominated by a major manufacturing concern with the work force divided into shifts. (This situation is quite common.) Assume the shift schedule is 7 a.m.-3 p.m. and that the average commute time to work is 15-20 minutes. In this situation you will have a worker who will probably wake at about 6:00 a.m., leave for work at about 6:40, and enter work at about 7:00. No amount of programming skill or tricks can extend that person's listening earlier than 6:00 nor later than 7:00. Under ideal circumstances, the person would rise to a clock radio at 6:00, have the radio on through dressing and breakfast for 40 minutes, and then pick up listening again while in transit to work from 6:40 until entering work at 7:00.

The maximum possibility is one hour a day for a five-day work week, or five hours a week. Compared against your station's Time Spent Listening computation, that maximum listening possibility would tell you a great deal about how well your programming is holding the audience. Obviously, if the maximum possibility was five hours and your Time Spent Listening was considerably shorter than that you might consider this as evidence that there is room for improvement.

In programming terms, computation of Time Spent Listening will give the programmer some idea of the time span he should program for in order to deliver the audience a complete package of information and music. Returning again to our example let's compute the Time Spent Listening for one day. Four hours × four quarter hours × Average Person (500) divided by Cume Persons (1500) = Time Spent Listening of 4 × 4 × 500 = 8000 divided by 1500 = 5.33 quarter hours or 1 hour and 20 minutes. In this case, the programmer has a full hour and 20 minutes each day to supply a balanced program of hit music, news, sports, weather, etc.

Suppose, however, that the Average Persons figure in our example had been 200 18-24 year-old men rather than 500. Our computation would now show that the programmer has only 31.9 minutes per day in which to supply a complete package of information to his listener. Accomplishing this may take the form of increased music rotation, shorter play list, more frequent newscasts, and greater repetition of information and service features.

In New York City, the all-news facility has a slogan that says something like "You give us 22 minutes and we'll give you the world." The station repeats a complete service of information every 22 minutes of the broadcast day. Programming experience tells me that the choice of 22 minutes was not accidental. I believe it was a skillful development drawn from an examination of the highly mobile mass transit-based commuter lifestyle of the New York City radio listener. It stands as a clear example of the usefulness of Time Spent Listening computations and audience turnover factors to the programmer.

Target Audience

We've been discussing computation of time spent listening by the audience. However, we seldom deal in radio with "the audience." What we deal with are a *number* of audiences. Fractionalization of format designs within the marketplace has created a fractionalization of audience segments. Many radio stations talk in terms of "target audience" as opposed to total audience.

A highly successful AOR (album oriented rock) format may talk of its audience goal as being 18-34 year-old adults for sales purposes. Realistically, however, the programmer may be aware that the format's primary appeal is to 18-24 year-old men. What he may need to know is not how much time the target audience group is listening, but how well his station is doing relative to other stations in the market in reaching the target audience.

In ARB terms this is called ETA—a measurement of *Efficiency of Target Audience*. It is computed by the following formula:

$$\text{ETA} = \frac{\text{Target Audience Time Spent Listening}}{\text{Total Audience Time Spent Listening}}$$

For an example, let's look at the 18-24 year-old men in the Harrisburg, Pennsylvania, April/May 1980 ARB diary, 3-7 p.m., Metro survey area. Station K shows the 18-24 male average quarter hour figure of 3 (300) and a cume of 54 (5400). Station S shows a quarter hour of 8 (800) and a cume of 71 (7100). The 3-7 time period contains 80 quarter hour segments. Using our Time Spent listening formulas, we compute the TSL for station K as 1 hour, 6½ minutes; for station S the TSL computes to 2 hours 15 minutes. We see that not only does station S have a larger audience than station K, but their audience listens longer.

What we're trying to find out, however, is how well our station is doing serving its target audience compared to its own total audience, so we need to do some further computations.

The ARB tells us that station K as an average audience 12+ of 36 (3600) and an average cume 12+ of 420 (42000). Station S has an average audience 12+ of 40 (4000) and a cume audience 12+ of 337

(33700). (All estimates in same daypart as original computations. If we compute the Time Spent Listening for the total audience, we develop the figures of 1 hour 43 minutes for station K and 2 hours 22½ minutes for station S. Now we can compare each station's ability to reach target audience, according to our ETA formula.

$$\text{ETA} = \frac{\text{Target Audience Time Spent Listening}}{\text{Total Audience Time Spent Listening}}$$

Station K: $\dfrac{4.44 \text{ gross quarter hours (Target Audience)}}{6.96 \text{ gross quarter hours (Total Audience)}} = .65$

Station S: $\dfrac{9.01 \text{ gross quarter hours (Target Audience)}}{9.50 \text{ gross quarter hours (Total Audience)}} = .95$

Comparing the two figures, we note that while neither station is as efficient in reaching this particular target demo as it is in reaching the total audience, station S is obviously doing a much better job that station K reaching the target in relation to total audience.

Using this same set of computations, you can evaluate the delivery of your station with relation to different audiences in various dayparts and measure your station's delivery as compared to any of your competitors.

Recycling

Another question that the ARB may indicate that the programmer should ask is "What percent of the listeners in one of my time periods also listen to my station in another time period?" This is often referred to as *recycling*. An understanding of this figure can be most important in attempting to determine how much of the AM drive audience returns for afternoon drive.

If the programmer were making plans to promote recycling of AM drive audience to FM, he might find that he already had 100% of his AM drive men recycled in the afternoon. Obviously his promotional effort in that set of circumstances would be considerably different than if the computation showed a low transference of audience.

The formula for computation of recycling is:

Percent Recycling = $\dfrac{\text{Cume audience that listens to both of two time periods}}{\text{Cume audience that listens to one of the time periods.}}$

Let's return to our Harrisburg example.

    Station K shows: 3800 men 6-10 a.m.
                           5400 men 3-7 p.m.

    Station S shows: 7800 men 6-10 a.m.
                           7100 men 3-7 p.m.

Added, we get:

        Station K: 9200 men 18-24
        Station S: 14900 men 18-24

ARB figures for combined drive time in that market indicate:

    Station K: 6000 men 18-24 (6-10 a.m. 3-7 p.m.)
    Station S: 7800 men 18-24 (6-10 a.m. 3-7 p.m.)

To find the recycling:

    Station K: 3800 men 6-10 a.m.
                   5400 men 3-7 p.m.
                 9200
                 6000 men (ARB combined drive)
                 3200 men in both drives

    Station S: 7800 men 6-10 a.m.
                 7100 men 3-7 p.m.
               14900
               7800 men (ARB combined drive)
               7100 men both drives

Recycling estimates:

$\dfrac{\text{Cume audience that listens to both of two time periods.}}{\text{Cume audience that listens to one of the time periods.}}$

Station K: $\dfrac{3200 \text{ men both periods}}{3800 \text{ men 6-10 a.m.}}$
                Percent of recycle: 84%

Station S: $\dfrac{7100 \text{ men both periods}}{7800 \text{ men 6-10 a.m.}}$
                Percent of recycle: 91%

Our conclusion is that on station K, of the 3800 men 18-24 who listen 6-10 a.m. in the Metro, 84% of them also listen in the afternoon drive from 3-7 p.m. On station S, of the 7800 men 18-24 who listen 6-10 a.m., 91% of them also listen to station S from 3-7 p.m.

Station S recycling percentage is significantly higher than station K although both seem to be doing well in recycling audience between drive periods.

Using the same system, percent of recycling can be compared among most dayparts among most audience compositions.

Available Audiences

Another important question for the programmer to ask is: "Which are the most available audiences during certain times of the day?" This estimate is particularly important in the demographic scheduling of music and of commercials. Audience mobility, working women, and other factors have destroyed the old concept that most men were available in morning and afternoon drive and only women are available 10-3.

The formula for computation of audience demographic by daypart is:

$$\text{Hour-by-hour demographic share} = \frac{\text{Target Audience}}{\text{Total 12+ audience}}$$

Again we'll look at Harrisburg, Pennsylvania, ARB hour-by-hour estimates, April/May '80, Mon.-Fri. 8:00-9:00 a.m. Metro Survey Area, Average Persons. What we see is this:

```
Total persons 12 +   103300
         Men   18-34   16000
       Women   18-34   16600
         Men   18-49   24000
       Women   18-49   30900
         Men   25-49   16100
       Women   25-49   25300
```

Using our formula, we determine:

$$\frac{\text{Target Audience}}{\text{Total 12+ Audience}} = \text{Hour-by-hour demographic share}$$

```
          Men   18-34: 15%
          Women 18-34: 16%
          Men   18-49: 23%
          Women 18-49: 30%
          Men   25-49: 16%
          Women 25-49: 24%
```

According to our assumption, there were more men available in morning drive than women... but according to our figures, there are more women available than men 8-9 a.m. in Harrisburg, Pennsylvania.

Let's look at an hour (2:00-3:00 p.m.) in the 10-3 daypart for comparison:

```
          Total Persons   12+    78400
          Men             18-34  14200   18%
          Women           18-34  14300   18%
          Men             18-49  22400   29%
          Women           18-49  20600   26%
          Men             25-49  15800   20%
          Women           25-49  14200   18%
```

If we held to the automatic assumption that women dominated radio listening mid-day (because the men are at work), our assumption fails in our actual example. Harrisburg has a substantial male listening audience through the mid-day time period.

We have concerned ourselves with some ARB terminology and formulas for extracting useful programming information from the ARB diary. Let's look at some additional terminology, not all of it related directly to ARB.

Survey Areas

Variation in rating results often occur when rating surveys are taken over different land mass or geographical area. All stations within a given radio market do not necessarily share either equal power or equal pattern direction. These variations alone mean that some stations will reach some parts of the population better than other stations in the same market. It may also mean that some stations will reach—or fail to reach—different parts of the land mass to be surveyed. It is therefore critical to understand the geographic boundaries of the survey and the relationship of the station or stations within the survey to the land mass as defined by their power output and signal definition.

The *Metro* or *Metro Survey Area* most often corresponds to an area's SMSA (Standard Metropolitan Statistical Area) or SCSA (Standard Consolidated Statistical Area) as defined by the U.S Government Department of Management and Budget. This area is a political definition based on marketing considerations (such as consumer buying patterns) and bears no direct relationship to radio station signals or power output within the Metro.

It is possible to have a station within a metro whose signal pattern is aimed away from the major Metro population distribution. This could happen because the definition of the station's signal pattern may have been made years before, based on a need to serve rural communities. As population developed within the area, the population may have moved to follow river beds, railroad tracks, natural land contours, or other criteria not related to the station's signal service pattern.

In some areas of the country where major cities may have SMSAs which are contiguous, the Metro may be defined as a "home county" of the major city or the surrounding townships to that city.

The *TSA (Total Survey Area)* differs from the Metro in that it is not either a political definition (such as a county) or a definition based on marketing patterns (SMSA). TSA is constructed from all Metro counties plus all other counties in which ARB finds significant listening to stations located in the Metro. Because of the reach and power of some stations in the Metro, it is possible for the TSA to include land mass far in excess of the power or signal pattern of many, or most, stations within the Metro. For example, WLS-Chicago is a 50,000 watt clear channel facility. It is often joked that for years WLS's TSA ranged as far away as Cleveland, Ohio, because WLS had significant and measurable listening in all of the Metro counties between Chicago and Cleveland. Obviously, the land mass was so great as to exclude just about all the stations competitive to WLS in the Chicago Metro from competing within the Chicago TSA.

The *ADI (Area of Dominant Influence)* and another survey designation known as *DMA (Designated Marketing Area)* reflect the signal reach of television stations in the Metro. The longer reach of television signals often make the ADI an unwieldy pattern for measurement of the small or medium-sized Metro stations. Why then, if many Metro stations can't reach the land mass covered by the ADI, would any rating service chose to utilize that large a survey area? The answer is twofold.

First, over much of the country, Metro surveys and TSA surveys still leave much of the population unmeasured. Obviously, in heavily rural areas with few population centers, the population which lies away from the population center may be served by no reasonable Metro or TSA designation which can take into account the limited power and signal pattern of small or medium stations. ADI allows ARB to measure those areas not covered otherwise.

Secondly, ADI is used by other media (such as newspapers, television, magazines, and outdoor) to measure audience. It is claimed that ADI gives radio an equal opportunity to compete for advertising dollars against these other media. It must be pointed out that the ADI is defined by television and that newspapers, magazines, and outdoor are not limited as to their reach and ability to match audience distribution patterns—as is radio.

An example of ADI problems happened in Connecticut when I worked at WPOP. The Hartford Metro contains CBS and NBC TV outlets. The ABC-TV outlet was in New Haven. The combined reach of the TV signals comprised an ADI which was virtually the whole state of Connecticut. However there are only a very few radio signals in Connecticut capable of covering the state. Measuring the listenership of radio stations in New Haven, Hartford, and Bridgeport according to ADI might produce some very strange results.

The *RSA (Pulse Radio Station Area)* is a geographical area constructed to include all counties surrounding the home city in which the central city stations achieve a 25% or greater daytime share of the audience. Other counties may be included so as to cover 90% of each station's weekly cume.

Powerful central city stations may have the long reach into outlying counties to garner themselves 25% of that county's daytime audience. Those counties may be so distant from the central city as not to include the signals of any of the lower-powered stations in that market.

The *Pulse Special Study Area* is a specially structured area designated by a specific station for whom the study is constructed. The station has the opportunity to gerrymander the special study area. The station's call letters included in the title of the survey usually warn of such attempts.

I can remember one station I worked for that commissioned a Special Study in an area which conformed exactly with our signal pattern. The results of that survey differed widely from the results indicated in either the Metro or the TSA for the market. (In this case the Metro chopped off the bottom half of our signal because the county ended four miles south of the station and the TSA covered a four county area in which we had almost no signal in two.) The special study provided information to merchants within our signal area as to the influence of our station in their particular township, with their customers. It provided us with a powerful selling tool.

Arbitron ESF

Among the new innovations in radio ratings services offered by Arbitron is the *Expanded Sample Frame*. Basically ESF is the inclusion, into the sample base, of unlisted telephone households. Since ARB participating households are contacted by phone to ascertain the willingness of the household to participate in a survey, unlisted telephone households were previously eliminated from the survey technique. With the Expanded Sample Frame, these households are now included and Arbitron feels "the sample population more accurately reflects the characteristics of the actual population and audience measurements have a higher reliability."

What is an unlisted household, and why is it unlisted? Unlisted households are simply telephone listings which do not appear in the telephone directory. These listings may be excluded from listing by request of the household or because the telephone listing came into being after the current telephone directory was printed. Arbitron has made provisions to cover both sets of circumstances.

Arbitron figures show that from a fifth to nearly half of the telephone households in various markets may be unlisted. Los Angeles is shown to have 46.9% of its phone listings in the unlisted household category. Figures show New York with 32.1%, Detroit with 40.2%, and Washington D.C. with 37.5%.

Similar percentage breakouts are indicated for most of the major metropolitan areas of the country. Obviously, a lot of people are covered in the "unlisted households" category.

Using computers, it is possible to construct a listing of possible numbers in a given exchange. In ARB literature the following example is used: Exchange PA5-12xx contains numbers ranging from PA5-1200 to PA5-1299. From this list of known possibilities the computer can deduct all of the numbers currently shown in the phone book. Those numbers not accounted for in the book, in this series, may be retained as "unlisted" numbers. From this list of numbers it is possible to program a systematic random sample which can be called. ARB also deletes all known commercial numbers and all numbers reserved for pay telephones from the numbers retained by the computer.

Respondents to unlisted numbers are handled in the same manner as respondents to listed numbers. An ARB field interviewer calls, asks if the respondent would care to participate in a survey and, if the answer is yes, determines the number of persons in the household 12 years or older. The household is sent a diary for each of these persons. Procedures for diary keeping, length of survey taken, etc., are the same for unlisted as for listed households.

The ESF reaches more audience, typically five to six percent more. Percentage changes for persons using radio within specific markets showed even more pronounced audience increase in some major metro markets.

Arbitron indicates that "experience is limited... single station inferences should not be drawn" from existing data. Obviously the effect ESF will have on an individual station or an individual format will depend on the extent to which there are unlisted households in the market and the socioeconomic makeup of that additional sample. As the data base increases, it is presumed that some predictions as to the effect of ESF on particular formats might be made. That information is not available at this time in such quantity as to make such predictions reliable.

WHAT LISTENERS DO WHILE THEY LISTEN

One of the basic concepts of radio programming is *repetition*—repetition of the station call letters (20-25 times per hour), the dial position (10-15 times per hour), your name (10-15 times per hour), record rotation, and saturation schedules for commercials. Radio is a frequency medium. Each play of each spot or bit of information reaches a part of the station's quarter hour audience figure.

There is more to it than that. Quarter hour and cume audience figures assume that the audience "listening" to your station is *listening* to your station. It assumes that people listen to radio with the same kind of attention they use when watching TV. Surveys don't substantiate that fact.

Figures compiled by the TGI (Target Group Index) indicate the following:

6:00-10:00 a.m.: 50.1% of U.S. adults listening to the radio do so while driving their cars; 36.6% are having breakfast, 32.1% have just awakened; 32.0% are showering or dressing; 28.1% are making breakfast; 21.7% relaxing; 14.0% working away from home; 4.6% other.

10:00 a.m-3:00 p.m.: 35.1% driving; 10.9% preparing meals; 19.2% eating; 18.8% listening; 17.5% relaxing; 16.1% working; 10.1% dressing; 9.7% doing laundry; 5.7% shopping; 4.6% doing yard or garden work; 4.0% other.

3:00-7:00 p.m.: 41.5% driving; 20.7% listening; 18.4% preparing meals; 17.3% relaxing; 10.5% dressing; 10.4% working; 7.7% entertaining; 4.3% other.

7:00-Midnight: 23.4% preparing to go to sleep; 22.0% driving; 16.8% relaxing; 14.7% listening; 10.4% working around the house; 9.7% eating; 9.1% dressing; 8.2% studying/reading; 7.5% entertaining; 4.8% cleaning; 4.0% other; 2.6% doing laundry.

Here are several important factors to consider:

☐ These figures represent only those people who have the radio on. It does not represent the masses of other people in the population who are watching television or participating in other forms of activity.

☐ Note the particularly high figures in all dayparts for the percentage of the audience that is driving. In-car audiences are an enormous percentage of the total listenership in all dayparts.

☐ The percentage of people who are just "listening" is highest from 10:00 a.m. to 7:00 p.m. Nothing is said about these people other than that they are adults. What assumptions can you draw about this listener?

☐ Obviously people's attention, when listening to radio, is divided. People listen to radio while engaged in other activities. What does this imply about attention span? What can you assume about their attention to any particular piece of business which has just happened on your station?

What assumptions can you draw about the tendency for radio to use repetition as a factor in reaching the audience?

LIFESTYLE RESEARCH

If you accept the premise that radio programming reflects our society and our times, then it follows that the more you know about each of these, the better you will be able to reflect. The use of sociological and psychological studies to forecast changes in attitudes, which may be reflected in program content, has been termed *lifestyle research*

To better understand lifestyle research let's consider some of the events which have lead up to the 1980s.

The 1960s were a decade of turmoil. Emerging social and ethnic groups created great pressures which burst forth as an extremely liberalized society. Massive changes in attitudes toward religion, politics, sex, and drugs took place in the '60s and these changes were mirrored by radio.

Radio newscasts were dominated by stories of riots, marches, sit-ins, sit-downs, takeovers, and assassinations. Music lyrics talked about sexual freedom and drugs as never before.

Personal lifestyles changed. Communal living and premarital cohabitation became commonplace. Longer hair, loose-fitting clothes, the no-bra look, and sandals replaced the jeans, poodle skirts, saddle shoes, and bouffant hair styles of the '50s.

Liberal attitudes changed the way we talked to each other on the radio. Rigid format radio, popular in the late '50s and early '60s, faded in popularity as radio began seeking "communicators" who could "relate" to the audience. The cry of the '60s was for freedom.

In the aftermath of the Vietnam war, Watergate, the new sexuality, and the '60s drug culture, researchers in the late 1970s began to forecast the rise of a new conservatism. It began as a knee-jerk reaction to the liberal '60s and developed into a major political and social force.

Shorter hair styles and fitted clothes were early evidences of conservative leanings. The law and order rhetoric of politics and startling Proposition 13 taxpayer revolt in California are solid evidence of conservative direction for the early '80s.

If radio was called upon to reflect the liberalism of the '60s in broadcast style, how will broadcasting reflect the conservatism of the '80s. What changes will be needed to reflect the socioeconomic climate of our times?

Anticipating these changes may provide the competitive edge for the '80s broadcaster. Programmers who wish to create and innovate need to keep close tabs on adjustments to the society. Lifestyle research will enable broadcasters to keep pace with change as it occurs. Programmers who fail to take lifestyle research into account will be playing "catch-up." In the 1980s, "catch-up" won't be good enough.

POPULATION PATTERN CHANGES

The biggest population phenomenon of the 20th century was the post-World War II birth rate, more popularly known as the "baby boom." Returning veterans, anxious to begin families, married and had children in the concentrated time frame following the end of the war. The "baby boom" created massive changes in our needs for goods, services, construction, and entertainment. Radio did not escape its effects.

To understand how the baby boom affected radio, let's look at the base year 1947 (two years following the end of the war in 1945). Let's look at what's happened to the ages of the babies born in the 1946-48 postwar period.

	Baby Boomers	*Postwar Teens*
1947	Birth	15 years old
1957	10 years old	25 years old
1967	20 years old	35 years old
1977	30 years old	45 years old
1980	33 years old	48 years old

The population bulge created by the baby boom has now become an audience in its early 30s. The postwar teens are now in their late 40s.

While overall population has been increasing, the birth rate has been declining. There are more of us, and we're living longer. This "aging" of the audience is a factor which radio must take into account.

Radio, which flourished as a teen appeal medium in the '50s and '60s now finds those same persons participating in entirely different lifestyles. The audience of the '50s and '60s now has concerns about family and career which were not present before. Radio stations which did not grow up with their audience have found themselves irrelevant.

As the '80s begin, we find an emphasis in radio on the "adult contemporary" format—a direct attempt to keep the rock heritage of the '50s and '60s and integrate it with the lifestyle concerns of the aging audience level.

Today's broadcaster faces a number of questions brought on by this age redistribution. What changes in broadcast styles and audience needs are predicted by this phenomenon? What does the aging audience pattern predict for the future of the youth-oriented format? How can the broadcaster prepare himself and his station to meet these audience changes?

Chapter 6
The Public Responsibility

When considering the granting of a license to operate a broadcast facility, the federal government charges the operator of the facility with the responsibility to operate in the public "interest, necessity, and convenience." The government feels it has the right to demand compliance with these criteria on the theory that the airwaves are the property of the public and the government is the custodian of the public's interest in that property.

In the real world of broadcast, I would suggest that the commitment to broadcast in the public "interest, necessity, and convenience" is rarely given day-to-day consideration. The government's mandated requirement that the public be advised of its right to challenge the licensee on the licensee's commitment to these criteria provides the only real spark of concern during the license term.

I do not imply that the operators of the license consciously avoid consideration of the "interest, necessity, and convenience" requirements. It is rather the fact that these requirements have never found proper definition that creates the problem.

What is the public "interest, necessity, and convenience?" Public radio and public television are supposedly operated solely with these commitments in mind and yet, in the main, the programming they offer is rejected by the public in favor of commercial broadcasters. The public hasn't shown much interest in what public broadcasters deem to be in the public "interest."

It could be argued that the broadcast facility which garners the largest audience does, by that very fact, satisfy the criteria. The willingness to listen or watch is the public's vote that the programming satisfies a need in their lives.

Who is to be the arbiter of the public interest? Who shall decide what constitutes necessity? Under the present system the licensee is required at license renewal to survey public "leaders" to determine the problems facing the community. They are further required to provide information on programming they have done, or plan to do, with regard to these community problems. Have we decided that the arbiters of the public's interest and necessity are the public's appointed or perceived leaders?

Those of us who have participated in the renewal process are aware that few leaders represent the public's interest. Each represents a *segment* of the public. Each is a lobbyist for the views of a minority interest. Religious, ethnic, and government representatives rarely attempt to represent the needs of *the* public, each represents the interests of *their* public. What the licensee eventually determines is a compilation of the interests of many "publics."

It is from this list of problems that the broadcaster devises his list of "community problems" and offers his plans for programming. It is against this list of perceived problems that his programming will be judged at the next renewal.

The definition of the public's "interest, necessity, and convenience" becomes the broadcaster's own definition measured against the separate definitions offered by those surveyed. To say the least, the system is flexible and open to interpretation. It is this very nature of imprecise definition which makes compliance with the criteria difficult.

AUDIENCE ACCEPTANCE AND PUBLIC SERVICE

What about audience levels? Do they play a part in our *public* responsibility? As I've pointed out before, it can be argued that audience acceptance alone may constitute some measurement of service.

In another view, the station that possesses the greatest capacity for public good is the station which has the greatest capacity for audience attraction. When the mass audience station turns its attention to a public problem, the greatest number of people become attuned to that problem. If a station has a social conscience, if it wishes to contribute to the community in a significant way, it should offer programming designed to attract a mass audience as an integral part of fulfilling that commitment to service. Whatever the social merit of the programming, the station must enlarge its capacity to attract an audience in order to enlarge its capacity to public contribution.

I have offered this same argument in discussing the case for popular music broadcasting before groups who charge that popular music stations do not offer "quality" programming. The capacity to attract a mass audience enables the popular music broadcaster to raise more money for charities, to attract audiences to public functions, to arouse public sympathy to community problems, and to get action from government. Because more people listen, more people can be motivated to respond.

I believe that mass appeal offers its own contribution to public responsibility.

Murray Lincoln, the first president of the Nationwide Insurance Companies, enunciated a credo that I believe serves us well. Mr. Lincoln suggested that business be able to answer two questions: What did you do for your community? And, did you make money? It is within the nature of our great radio medium to develop a tremendous capacity for motivating people to action. Control over that capacity brings with it a responsibility to use our ability to motivate for the public good. What did you do for your community? How did you use the capacity of your station to motivate action to contribute to your community?

In answering these questions you will have gone a long way toward fulfilling your public responsibility. Inability to provide a satisfactory answer says something about your contribution beyond the measurement of public "interest, necessity, and convenience." An unsatisfactory answer says you lack a public conscience.

In order to perform our public responsibility it is inherent that we maintain fiscal responsibility. Did you make money? Public performance without creditable fiscal performance offers no opportunity for continuum. Fiscally unsound ventures are doomed to failure and failure interrupts your public contribution.

There is neither shame nor wrong in the profit motive. Profit provides the means of funding the public good. If there is a wrong in profit, it is in the dissemination of the profits, not in their making. Failure to use profits to increase the quality of life is the only shame.

THE LOTTERY LAW

This section offers a brief examination of *lottery* and what constitutes a lottery as it applies to broadcast. (For a more detailed examination of this important subject readers are urged to secure from the National Association of Broadcasters, 1771 N. St. N.W., Washington, D.C. 20036, a copy of their excellent booklet entitled, *Broadcasting and the Federal Lottery Laws*. This booklet provides detailed explanations and examples of lottery and commission rulings in a number of different kinds of cases.)

We will discuss lottery as the most common form of problem to be found in station or client contests and offers.

To constitute a lottery, the promotion or contest must contain three basic elements: *prize, chance,* and *consideration.* All three of these elements must be present to constitute a finding that a lottery is present. If any element is lacking, the promotion or contest may be held not to be a lottery. Every promotion or contest must then be evaluated in these terms.

Prize: Is there a prize? Will the player win something in the promotion? It may be a physical item, or it may be a "discount" on a purchase. This is usually the easiest element of lottery to determine. Obviously, if there is no prize, there is no lottery.

Chance: If the player has an opportunity to win or lose, the element of chance is probably present. If the contest involves guessing the number of something, or being drawn from a hat, chosen by the spin of a wheel, or predicting the outcome of an event, chance is present.

Chance is also present if the *amount* of the prize is determined by chance. One of the most famous of these promotions is called "Money Tree." In this promotion a customer enters the showroom and selects an envelope from the Money Tree. After purchasing an item, the envelope is opened and the "discount" off the purchase price is determined from information contained in the envelope. (In the case of auto dealers, the envelope may contain discounts ranging from $50 to $500.) Although everyone who plays wins, the element of chance is still present because the *amount* of the prize is determined by chance choice from the Money Tree.

When is chance *not* present? Chance is not present when the winner of the contest is determined entirely and solely by the use of skill. However, it has been held that even in contests of skill, chance may be present if the contest operator has failed to announce or publish the rules or standards for judging or if the contest operator has waived or violated those rules in the judging.

In setting up promotional contests for your station in which you intend to establish the winner by skill, it is wise to consult with the station attorney on all contest rules and judging standards before airing the contest.

Consideration: This is the most "dangerous" area of the lottery law. It is the area in which most gray area cases are found. *Consideration* may be present if any of three sets of conditions are present.

☐ If the contestant is required to "furnish any money or thing of value."
☐ If the contestant must have in his/her possession any product sold, furnished, or distributed by a sponsor,
☐ If the contest involves a "substantial expenditure of time and effort" by the contestant.

Money or thing of value: It is generally easy to ascertain whether the contestant is required to fulfill this requirement. If the contestant is required to make a purchase to participate in the contest, the element of consideration is present.

Possession of any product sold, furnished or distributed by the sponsor: Contests involving sending in box tops or other items requiring purchase of a product constitute consideration. If, however, the item is provided without cost or obligation to the contestant, the question is arguable. If the case for possession can be circumvented, as in the case where box tops may be replaced by "reasonable facsimilies" on plain paper, consideration may be ruled not to be present. In the case where purchasers and non-purchasers of the product are allowed to enter the contest, the chance to win must be equal between purchasers and non-purchasers in order for a ruling of "no consideration" to be found.

Example: Publishers' Clearing House advertises in the broadcast media. In their contact with the audience they urge the audience to take advantage of huge savings on magazine purchases. Hundreds of thousands of dollars in prizes are offered, from entries to be drawn at random. The entry blank clearly provides, as it must, an opportunity for the contestant to enter without purchasing any magazines at all. Entries from purchasers and non-purchasers must be given the same opportunity to be drawn.

Substantial expenditure of time and effort: This is another gray area. Merely requiring the contestant to go to a particular location to obtain an entry form has been held not to constitute substantial expenditure of time and effort. If the time and place of the drawing are clearly promoted, requiring presence at the drawing has been held not to constitute consideration. However, suppose the time and place of the drawing is somewhat distant from the contestant.

Does the expenditure of time, effort, and travel expense to get to the location constitute consideration?

Suppose your station were broadcasting from within a state fair or a theater and you held a contest. Those persons coming to your broadcast booth could register to win a new car. Prize is present; chance is present. Everybody who comes to the booth may enter. There is nothing to purchase, nothing to possess, no special expenditure of time and effort required. You would rule no consideration. However, what if the state fair or the theater has an admission fee? Persons who did not pay the admission could not participate. Is consideration present?

In this case, consideration would probably be ruled not present. Consideration did not pass *between the parties involved in the contest*. Consideration passed between the contestant and the operator of the fair or the theater. The station did not participate in the consideration.

Suppose, however, that in drawing up the plans for participation in the fair by the station, the contest was discussed with the fair or theater operator as a method to draw customers to the event. If this element were an implicit or implied part of the station presence or participation in the event, the station could be held to be a party to the consideration.

Assume that the exhibitors to the fair are charged for booth space. Assume too that the station's charge for booth space is waived by the promoter because he considers your presence advertising for his event. Is the waiving of the space cost held as a separate transaction between the parties or does it make the station a participant in the event? The answer to that question would have a bearing on the subject of *to whom* and *between whom* did consideration pass.

It should be clear that the lottery law applies to client promotions and contests as well as to station-sponsored events. The station may be held liable for lottery in a client-operated promotion contained entirely within the client's commercial spot schedule. The program director is responsible to determine the facts before allowing broadcast of a client promotion which may be suspect.

Before broadcasting any promotion or contests, ask the following questions:

☐ Is there a prize?
☐ Will the winner be chosen on the basis of skill or chance?
☐ What does the contestant have to do to play?

All on-air contests should be carefully documented as to rules controlling participation, judging, and winning. Rules should be cleared with station legal experts prior to broadcast.

If a client promotion is suspect, the promotion must be held off the air until the answers to the questions regarding lottery are determined.

HANDLING COMPLAINTS

Letters to the radio station with compliments or complaints become part of the station's public file. This file must be made available to the public for examination.

Complaint letters should be answered within 24 hours of receipt. Your response must also be filed in the public file.

Let's look at the kind of complaint which can cause problems. At one station I worked, we were doing a commercial for a sponsor promotion which indicated that everyone who came in to a sponsor location and purchased a bucket of chicken would be given a T-shirt. A listener went to a sponsor location, bought a bucket of chicken, asked for her T-shirt, and was told by the store manager that they had run out of T-shirts. Driving away from the location, the listener heard our station run the commercial again and promised a T-shirt purchase of a bucket of chicken.

Angered, the listener filed a complaint with the FCC charging the station with "false and misleading" advertising. The FCC forwarded the complaint to the Federal Trade Commission for their consideration.

When we were notified of the complaint we contacted our station's legal firm and the problem was given to me to work out.

If the supply of T-shirts had run out, it could indicate that the sponsor never had enough T-shirts to accommodate the expected demand. If that were true, and the station failed to ascertain that fact in advance and qualify the offer on the air, the station could be liable as charged.

In this case, I determined that the sponsor was well prepared with enough T-shirts to satisfy the anticipated demand. However, the supply of shirts *at that location* had run out. The listener had come in for her purchase before an additional supply could be ferried to that location from the warehouse.

The "fault" lies in the failure of the store manager to notify the purchaser of that fact and to take the listener's name and address so that a T-shirt could be forwarded.

Even though I determined the station was not at fault, we would have to deal with the complaint unless it was withdrawn. We could have had to go to an FCC hearing on the matter, with the resultant legal cost.

We avoided having to face a hearing when I phoned the complainant, discussed the problem, offered an explanation, and made good her loss by supplying not only the client's T-shirt but several of our own station T-shirts as well. In return, I requested that she draft a letter withdrawing her complaint. She did so and I sent it off to our legal staff, with copies for our file and the FTC and FCC.

The important point is that the program director must be aware of the fact that the station may be held liable not only for its own actions, but for the actions of others when it broadcasts information regarding those actions. It is obvious that the station should be held responsible for running improperly supervised or illegal contests. The station is also liable for impropriety and illegality in sponsor contests if the information is promoted on the air. Should those improprieties or illegalities result in a listener complaint, you will be responsible to answer for them in 24 hours. The responsibility for awareness is yours.

THE OMBUDSMAN

Service to the community is more than a mandated requirement to many radio stations. Community service is a commitment the station seeks to fulfill. One of the most useful forms of such service may be found in the concept known as the *ombudsman*.

In effect, the ombudsman is a "people's watchdog." Although the ombudsman has no official standing, the concept has behind it the power of the press and the threat of public exposure to make its pressure felt. It works as follows:

Station X appoints a person, perhaps a newsman, to be identified as the ombudsman. Letters to the station are solicited describing problems listeners face and an offer is made to help solve some of these problems. Letters with unique problems of community interest or universal appeal are selected for action by the ombudsman.

One caution: Many of the letters submitted will be without merit. The station must establish the legitimacy of the claimant's claim. Many situations suggested will be by persons who have not exhausted legal remedies or for whom legal remedies may be the only reasonable solution. The station cannot become involved in such cases. After facts have been determined and the letter qualified, the station ombudsman may take an interest in the problem. Sample problems which can be tackled are:

- Efforts to secure traffic lights at dangerous intersections or school crosswalks.
- Failure of 911 Emergency Line operators to respond quickly, or correctly, to situations (such a situation just came up in New York City).
- Slow responses by ambulance companies to emergency calls (such a situation was also recently documented in New York City).
- Warranty/guarantee/money-back offers on products. WWBT-television, Richmond, Virginia, did this most successfully with a "Tell It To Doug (Hill)" feature in the nightly news.
- Pollution observations by listeners. A major problem with a cancer-causing agent called Kepone was brought to the media's attention this way several years ago. It led to a major government investigation.

The ombudsman may respond to problems in two ways. He may make referrals to government or social agencies, or he may make a call on behalf of the complainant and attempt to encourage a positive result.

Feature broadcasts with the ombudsman, outlining the specific problem and making clear that, due to the intercession of your station, the problem is now on the way to being solved, add to your public service.

The ombudsman concept was extended by WMCA, New York, in a program called "Call for Action." (Full details are available from WMCA on how your station can initiate a "Call for Action" program.) The basics of the concept are the same except that in "Call for Action" the station may work through a local civic group. Facilities are provided for a woman's group to monitor phones during a specific set of times. Calls are solicited. Cross-index files of information regarding governmental or social agencies handling every sort of problem are kept. Referrals for problem solutions are made.

A specified period later (30-60 days), follow-up calls are made to the complainant to determine results. Files are updated constantly to assure accurate referrals.

Special ombudsman phone lines can be developed to respond to immediate community problems such as lack of heat at listener homes or gasoline shortages.

The ombudsman concept provides an active way for the station to become involved in the community with a meaningful public service.

Chapter 7
Random Observations

Success is seldom accomplished without a solid grounding in philosophy. Success itself is the product of philosophical approach.

THOUGHTS ON SUCCESS

We do not intend to offer a course in the philosophical approach to programming. We do have some thoughts on the matter we would like to share.

Patience

As the old sayings go, "patience is a virtue" and "haste makes waste." In programming, these may be valuable pieces of advice.

Radio programming is an evolutionary, rather than revolutionary, process. Audiences seek an identity with the station sound. Because the medium is projected into their homes, audiences seek a familiarity with their guests." Quick changes in programming create audience trauma. Changes upset the balance of identity between the audience and the station. Unless you are prepared to provide a heavy promotional campaign to explain and justify the change, your audience may feel dislocated from familiar surroundings. They may turn to another station to regain the familiar.

Plan programming for the long haul. Establish familiar listening patterns, familiar format patterns, familiar music patterns. Minimize audience trauma. Plan and execute changes while maintaining a familiar station sound.

Think

Programming requires concentration. Think ahead, innovate, create, avoid counterprogramming. Counterprogramming is unproductive. Counterprogramming lacks innovation. Counterprogramming subverts creativity.

Spend some time each day in reflection. Evaluate how what you've done contributed to your goals. Think about how what you plan to do contributes to your goals. Plan your work, and work your plan.

Hustle

In a competitive business another old adage may be relevant: "He who hesitates is lost." Do it *now*! Putting something off until tomorrow may mean the competition will do it today. The competition isn't waiting on you. If you're behind, hustle to catch up. If you're number one, hustle to stay there. Above all, don't be afraid to compete.

Know Where You're Going

Set goals. You can't get there if you don't know where you are going. What is it you want to accomplish during this rating period? What are your target demographics in each daypart? Are your goals reasonable?

What's the Price?

Goal attainment has a price. It may be time, energy, training, money, or something totally unexpected. There are no free rides. Failure to determine the price will lead to failure. What do you have to do; to whom do you have to appeal to attain your goals? Do you have to change the music, hire a new staff, create an exciting contest, or spend money on promotion? *What is the price?*

Pay the Price

It's called "paying dues." The "lucky break," the "overnight" success, usually comes to the prepared. If you think the price is too high, be prepared not to attain all of your goals.

If the price of attracting a teen audience at night is a new jock, pay it. If loyalties prevent you from replacing a friend, be prepared to fail.

If the price can be paid in material goods, it's probably cheap. Paying the price in emotional wares is the difficult assignment.

Know your goal, find out what you have to do to fulfill it, then *do it*.

Who Are You, and Where Are You Going?

When I attended the University of Rhode Island, I had a professor who based most of the grades he handed out on the answers he received to these two questions. His students were asked the questions at the beginning of the course, and again at the end. Grades depended upon the "growth" shown between the two sets of answers to the same questions.

Who am I? Most of us would begin with a physical description but physical descriptions don't answer *who*, physical descriptions answer *what*. *Who am I?* What is it that *is* what *I am*?

Where am I going? The answer is not to be found in a description of career goals. They are the answer to "What do I want to do for a living?" Where am I going?

Success is elusive and success is difficult to define. The definition varies for each individual. For some, success can be measured in monetary terms; for others it may be found in satisfaction. Whatever success is for you, understanding what it is becomes a major part of its attainment.

ASK ME

There is a sales concept we should all pick up which is adaptable to many programming situations. It's called the "ask me" call.

In this situation, the salesman calls on the client and makes *no attempt to sell*. The purpose of the call is to learn something about the client's business. Then the salesman goes back to his office to determine what he can do for the client. He drafts a proposal that will make the client's business better and takes it back to the client on a second call.

Think of the audience as your client. Spend some time finding out what your client, the audience, wants and needs. Design your programming to meet those needs. Give the audience what it wants and needs, rather than your preconceived notions about what you planned to "sell." The results may be quite different from your original plan but it will serve your community better and gain you more listeners.

PITFALLS TO AVOID

Some people succeed, some people fail. Failure can be a good teacher. Understanding *why* you failed may lead to corrective steps. We thought we might look at some of the causes for failure, some of the pitfalls to avoid.

Overconfidence: When you think you are the strongest, you are most vulnerable. Overconfidence may mean you underestimate the competition. It may mean you've taken the audience for granted. It may mean you've relaxed your vigil.

A very famous program director at a most successful station spent every afternoon during a rating book on the golf course. His superior signal was beaten in that rating by a much smaller station. Of course it was a fluke brought on by a program director who was overconfident, but that fluke took six months—until the next rating book—to correct. In the meantime, the station lost considerable revenue.

Competition: Every year the competition changes. Radio stations compete with other stations in the same market but competition may be from other sources as well. Television, the growth of leisure time activities, changes in lifestyles—all take audience away from radio or change listening patterns and habits. Failure to be aware of all kinds and types of competition can lead to disaster. You may be programming to the wrong people, at the wrong times.

Lack of rapport: Someone once said that nobody ever went broke underestimating the American public. However, underestimating your rapport with the audience can be fatal. You begin talking *at* the audience and not *to* the audience. You become so involved with programming that you become insulate and lose sensitivity to audience needs.

Audience mobility: The audience is not a static thing. Every year it gets older; every year part of the audience moves away from your broadcast area. Some of the audience marry; substantial changes occur in their lifestyle. The subtle shifting of audience patterns can destroy a successful station that fails to adjust to the changes. Mobility decreases audience loyalty. You must constantly promote to reinforce loyalty.

You fail to grow: Radio is a reactive medium. Radio reacts to changes in the community. When you become so confident of your position that you fail to innovate, you invite failure. Innovation is a key to remaining fresh and vital. Listen to your station. If you can predict the next thing that's going to happen, you may already have become stale.

Pride: Be proud of your station but do not overlook your shortcomings. These are areas of potential growth.

Goals: Set attainable short and long-term goals. Goals provide a benchmark against which to measure progress. Without a way to measure progress, there is no way to measure slippage.

Fear: Fear uses up energy, burns up creativity, results in make-work projects, and contributes nothing to success. Fear often results in counterprogramming and destroys your ability to lead.

Localization: Your radio station is part of your local community. It is not part of the major market to which you aspire. Program for your local community. Instantaneous national communication can now reach every corner of every rural community. Your local audience has access to television, magazines, and films that vastly increase their awareness of events and cultures. Your contribution can best be made by demonstrating how these events affect your local community. Translate the big picture into real terms on a local level.

Involvement: There is no substitution for your own personal involvement with every aspect of your programming. As a program director you can be the catalyst that keeps the elements fresh. When you become too involved in mechanics, you fail to act as a catalyst. Remember, your role is leadership.

COMPUTERS IN PROGRAMMING

Although we have the facilities today to completely automate programming with computers, the cost factor involved makes computer programming unrealistic in anything but major markets. There are some computer functions which are feasible for smaller markets; let's take a look at some of these.

One system (Compunet) enables the client station to utilize a master computer on a time-share basis. The program director contributes to this function by providing the computer with every element of his format for every hour of the broadcast week. The computer is given instructions as to placement of news, weather, PSAs, commercial spot sets, commercial content restrictions per hour, contest play placement, special programs, and whatever else the format contains. Once set into the computer, these elements will repeat each week with regularity.

Continuity departments enter the daily commercial content into the computer along with scheduling information. Commercial content is identified by codes with regard to client name, competitive product identification, spot price, time preference, and salesman. The computer sorts the spots for placement in each hour. Spots are entered according to the number of total commercial minutes or units specified by the format. Competitive product separation is maintained. Spots may be entered according to dollar value, with higher-priced spots having priority over lower-priced spots. This maximizes the value of each day's log.

What results each day is a completed log containing all format items and all commercial content, entirely computer programmed and balanced.

Computerization also allows management to pull daily reports from the log by daypart, by salesman, by client, and by dollar value. Since spot schedules are entered for the whole run, the continuity department need deal with each schedule only once. Projections can be developed for log values by day, week, month, or salesman. Such projections are of great value to management in planning promotion expenditures and to programming in planning promotions.

Computerization means automatic billing for each client at the end of the broadcast month.

Changes in format items, addition of program elements, and alterations in the log form can be done with simple computer entries.

Computers in Music Programming

There are a number of music programming systems available on computer. In the most sophisticated of these, the computer is capable of programming the entire music balance of the station automatically, taking into account demographic appeal, pacing, and rotation.

In a simplified system, each title is entered into the computer. Each title is coded as to the demographic appeal of the song and the specific rotation the program director desires. (Example: Song is entered. Computer is told the song appeals to 18-24 year-old females and is not to be repeated more than once every two weeks as a Golden.)

In setting up his music program, the air personality is given a music format sheet. The sheet may call for music appeal to specific demographic groups the station wishes to attract to his program. If the format sheet calls for a Golden appealing to 18-24 year-old females, he punches that into the computer. The screen reads out a number of titles available in that demo. He makes a choice from the available group and indicates it to the computer. That title disappears from the screen and cannot be recalled again for at least two weeks.

In a fully automated system, all the music may be contained on reels which automatically cue as the songs are selected. The air personality never sees the records or cartridges.

Computers in the Control Room

In one new system the air personality never handles the broadcast log. As he needs information, he has the log flashed on a computer screen in the control room. As he completes each element he "writes" on the screen to indicate completion. The computer reads the pen and automatically files the information. The log, when printed, is a completed log with all elements available for manual rechecking.

Computer Engineering

Some stations have automatic computer adjustment and logging of engineering data. The computer is in control of various engineering variables. Should the signal drift, the computer makes a correction. Readings are taken every half-hour and logged. Engineers need only check the computer tape and sign the log.

Although fully computerized programming systems are available, it will be some time before such systems are within the financial reach of most stations. It is entirely possible that the medium market program director of today will have to deal with some form of computerization. A familiarity with the possibilities is a first step to command of these systems.

Appendix
Interviews on
Successful Programming

One of the great pleasures of the radio business is that it is truly a small world. We work within the framework of a limited number of radio stations and an even smaller number of chain ownership operations which keep crossing our paths. We have the facility of mobility and enjoy a free exchange of ideas and communication that shrinks our universe further.

The inevitable result of such communication is that some of the people we meet, we become friends with and know for a long period of time.

In this section I would like to introduce you to some of my friends. In his own way each has had an effect on our business and each has some interesting stories to tell.

Ken Wolt

I knew Ken Wolt when he was programming WPOP Radio in Hartford, Connecticut as Dan Clayton. Clayton is best remembered as being a man constantly at the center of a whirlwind... which was often of his own creation.

As a program director he demanded a letter-perfect execution of his format. As a disk jocket he often broke most of his own rules.

As a person Clayton constantly strove for personal development. I remember very well being invited to his home and taking the opportunity to study his library. Where you expected to find Mikey Spillaine you found Shakespeare. He is a man surprisingly well read in the classics who seems to have an outward reluctance to have that perceived. In the face of heavy work schedules, Clayton always found time to take courses at colleges... and it did not surprise me to find that he continues that practice to this day.

I have a great deal of respect for Clayton/Wolt, have celebrated in his achievements and predict that Ken Wolt will be a force in broadcasting for some time to come.

Q. *You've had a pretty distinguished career in radio to date. Will you trace for us your background in radio. Where did you start, where did you progress to and how did you grow in title?*

A. I started in radio as a disk jockey in high school in Mount Vernon, Washington, which had the only radio station near Sedro Valley, my hometown. After joining the service, I helped put a station on the air in Japan for the Far East Network and did a disk jockey show that was broadcast to the servicemen on duty aboard ship in the Far East. I was on the network as an afternoon disk jockey.

When I came back to the United States I went to college at San Diego State and wanted to become an electronics engineer. I worked part-time at several stations in San Diego. I found it difficult to find a full-time job because of the training given in the military—it wasn't considered adequate.

After I got out of college I got a job at Astronautics working on the Atlas missile as an electronics engineer. After six months I found it to be the most boring thing I've ever dreamed possible and went out to try to get back into radio. I got a job at EEAU in Tiajuana under the name of Lucky Night. It was interesting because the station in Mexico couldn't be owned by an American, so we leased time from the Mexican owner and broadcast country music.

The morning man was a guy by the name of Smokey Rogers, and I did news for him to begin with and later got my own disk jockey show. We would broadcast from 8:00 to 12:00 noon to start with and 8:00 p.m. to 6:00 a.m., and finally we went 18 hours a day. The station was really terrible. There was no air conditioning; the windows were open for a little cooling, and goats and cows would stick their heads in at the most inopportune times.

From there I went to Las Vegas. I got a job as a morning man at KENO using the name of Coffee Jim Dandy. I did mornings from 1962 to 1966. We had amazing numbers; we did crazy things. As the name would imply, Coffee Jim was really a featherhead and we did a lot of fun, dumb things. We didn't know any better. The audience was really entertained and enjoyed it and responded well. We had a 70 share on one of the polls out there. We were the number one station after six months, and it stayed that way until I left. I guess it still is.

I left KENO in 1966, after the sale of the station. I just felt my career in Las Vegas was stymied, and I really wanted to try to hit the big time as a jock. I went to Denver, and was renamed by the manager, Ev Wren, after one of his favorite disk jockeys in a town in Missouri. He called me Dan Clayton. That name stuck with me from '66 to 1979.

From Denver I made a brief stop in Washington at WPGC and ended up in Hartford, Connecticut on WPOP doing afternoons, still using the name

Dan Clayton. After six or eight months I was named program director of WPOP and retained that title until 1969.

I went from Hartford to Phoenix, Arizona, at KRIZ, as National Program Director for Doubleday Broadcasting, operating out of the station.

I was in Phoenix for a little over a year when I heard of an opening in Cincinnati at WLW, one of America's great radio stations. I applied for it. I was there for about six months and was named program director. This was in 1970. I stayed at WLW from 1970 to 1973 as PD. I left the air after a year and a half. I had to make a choice. A station like WLW had so many managerial responsibilities that it was just physically impossible for me to go on the air. I was working 18 hours a day trying to keep all the loose ends tied—I did the music, all the promotions, all the contests, all the scheduling (baseball, hockey, helicopter weather) *plus* a four-hour afternoon shift. It was a killer. After a year and a half I couldn't take it anymore. I had to make a decision. Was I going to continue to try to be a disk jockey for the rest of my life—did that really satisfy me?—or should I try to get into management? I opted for the latter. I hired a fellow named Bob Beasley from Chicago as my replacement in afternoon drive and became full-time program director at WLW.

In 1973 I was contacted by NBC. They were having rating troubles in Washington, D.C. at their O & O station WRC and they offered me a job. It seemed like a great challenge, so I took the job. At WRC I really had some remarkable success, mainly because of timing. The previous program director had changed the entire staff and had tried to change the station from old line MOR to adult contemporary. He spent thousands and thousands of dollars, and the ratings went down. However, what they had done was clean out all the old-line image people that they had on staff, and that made my job easier. We went in and in one book, less than six months, took the station from number 17 to number one in 18-34 adults, number two in teens, and number two overall in Washington—a phenomenal success. After being in Washington for some time, things were going along well and the station was making money for the first time in years. It occurred to me that I was doing the same kinds of things in Washington in 1973-74 that I had done in Las Vegas and Hartford in 1965-66. I was using basically the same record rotation. I used a pretty sophisticated rotation system, but once you do it it works pretty well. It's tough to get jocks up for a "Jock in the Box" contest for the umpteenth time. In short, I found myself—and maybe if we hadn't had such great success in Washington I might not have felt the same—getting bored. I started looking around. I had known as early as Hartford five or six years earlier, that I wanted to be the general manager of a station.

The stock answer given to me was that general managers always come from the sales department and that the program director was usually, by the Peter Principle, the best disk jockey. You kind of worked your way up through the ranks. I decided that I was going to prepare myself as best I could, considering my limited knowledge as to exactly what the job of

General Manager entailed. In 1974 I started looking into such things as FCC regulations, engineering, philosophies, budgets, personnel motivation, and other related areas. However I never had full grasp of the job until I got it.

In 1973 I was contacted by Dave Klemm from Blair radio who suggested that there was a job opening with an organization called LIN Broadcasting, and that I should explore it with the vice-president who was at that time running WAKY in Louisville) Don Meyers. To make a long story short, I was given a lot of tests, interviewed a number of times, and won the job in February, 1974, as general manager and president of WBBF, Rochester, N.Y.

Q. *At a time when most general managers were being promoted from the ranks of the sales department, you came up through the programming ranks. You have detailed some of the things you did to prepare for the promotion. What did you do about sales training?*

A. All the years I spent as a program director gave me insight into the organization and operation of radio stations. The experience at WLW and NBC was invaluable in terms of operating with a large number of people, having the responsibility of directing a large staff, etc. I didn't have any specific sales training.

Q. *What would you say was the most difficult problem you faced in adjusting to the role of general manager?*

A. My most difficult problem was relegating programming to its proper role and doing the same for sales. The two departments have to coexist and sometimes as a general manager I had to make a decision in favor of sales over programming, even though it came as foreign to my nature. For the first time I was faced with the problem of supporting a lot of people who depended on me for their livelihood and it was a large responsibility. Not only was I responsible for bringing home the bacon, but also more acutely aware than even the sales manager that you can't kill the goose to do so. It was, and is, the most difficult problem I encounter every day.

Q. *The temptation to involve yourself in programming decisions must be great, since you were a programmer. Were you able, are you able, to remove yourself from programming or do you find yourself being drawn into day-by-day programming decisions?*

A. I find myself very involved in all major programming decisions. I don't decide whether we go on a new record. I don't decide whether a jingle should follow a promo, etc. I do get involved with overall planning strategy and direction of every facet of the radio station. I find myself very involved with what contests we run, what promotions we air, what audience we are targeting on, what jingle package we buy, and so forth. However, I am also very involved with the day-to-day pricing of the station, what sales packages we offer, what sales promotions we do and how involved we get with sponsors. In addition, I regularly find myself in the car driving the signal with the chief engineer, and recently went out to help weld a ground strap for our AM antenna project. The general manager must be aware of *every* facet of the radio station, although he can't be expected, or can't expect, to be involved with everyday running of the departments.

Q. *If you met someone in programming who wanted promotion to general manager, what advice would you give him on how to prepare for the challenges of the job?*

A. I would say that he/she should go to a Welch or an RAB sales school. I think you should get as many human behavior/motivational experiences and courses as possible. The Dale Carnegie course comes to mind. Understanding the kind of problems other people are going to present you with is important, because frankly, at this station I've got 60 people who work here and there are 69 problems. Everybody's got a problem of their own that they hit you with as you walk in the door and that's what takes up most of my time.

Any financial education you can get would be helpful, such as accounting. I've gone back to college myself. I'm presently taking night courses at Perdue and it's tough.

I might tell you about a personal experience that's not too far off our subject. When I got the job as general manager in Rochester I was interviewed for it at WAKY in Louisville. The day I signed the contract the vice president of the corporation handed me the month's operating statement. Attached to it was the budget for the year. I'd seen budgets before but I'd never been schooled on them. I'd never been trained on how to interpret what the numbers meant. There were pages and pages of figures. I didn't want to admit that I couldn't read the figures so I tried to bluff my way through. "Look at those expenses," he said. "That's really something," said I. "Look at that profit." "That's really something," said I. "That really stinks" said he. "Yeah, that's terrible," said I. To tell you the truth I hadn't the faintest idea whether it was bad or good. Whatever he said, it must have been right. That's the kind of thing that every program director who walks into a general manager's job is faced with. What does all this stuff mean? I went over those operating statements until I was confident that should anybody ask me any questions, I knew what every line stood for. I was up a lot of nights studying those reports.

Q. *In Indianapolis, you are responsible for an AM (WNDE) and an FM (WFBQ). Much has been said about the differences between the AM and the FM audience. Do you see a difference between the audience for AM and the audience for FM and can you tell us what they are?*

It's an interesting question. I don't think there is a difference in the audience; I think the difference is in the way the stations are consumed. I think the difference is in what is presented—in what the audience needs, by daypart. In the morning, FM stations have gotten themselves into a kind of a box. People know that if they listen to FM in the morning they'll never get any news, any information or any sports. FM stations have conditioned people to expect that. I think if you put an FM station on with the services that AM provides, in stereo, with the right promotion, you'd knock 'em dead ... but who has the guts to do that? Our own FM is "Superstars" AOR and that audience isn't attracted to full-service programming.

In terms of your question it depends upon what you're talking about daypart-wise. My AM doesn't only share audience with my FM but with all FM stations ... afternoons and evenings. They listen to us for things that are important to them when that information is available—traffic, news, sports etc. They listen to FM when the services it offers are important to them.

Q. *As a general manager you are concerned not only with your stations today, but must prepare them for the future. What do you see as the future for AM and for FM radio? Do you agree that FM will be the "music" medium or "entertainment" medium as AM becomes the "information" medium?*

A. I think we're talking in terms of semantics. I would say that it depends on what you consider "entertainment." I don't think that FM will be the entertainment medium; I don't think they are now. I think they are a music medium and I think they will continue to do that, to be that. I don't think they have a lock on the boards when it comes to entertainment. When I say entertainment, I'm talking about personalities, I'm talking about theater. I think those are still AM entities. I think that if AM would take the horse by the reins (which we are doing with some success at WNDE) as far as making an effort to make radio interesting or funny or entertaining, AM would make a comeback. We've doubled our numbers on AM. Some of them came from other AM stations, but a lot of them came from FM. They listen to us for what is offered when that sort of thing is important. We doubled our numbers in every daypart—until it came to nights. When we offered the same sort of fare it stayed flat; we didn't move at all. I think that AM may become *more* entertainment-oriented. I think you'll see a comeback of the one-liners, the voice tracks ... and the crazies. I think there is a need for them. There is no "fun" in radio anymore. When you get guys like Don Imus who are really strong personalities—although not only offered in mornings although that sort of programming is traditional and expected in mornings—you bring entertainment back into radio.

Q. *The FCC is considering expansion of the AM dial to provide access to many more facilities. It has also suggested the elimination of the clear channel designation and reduction of power to the 50 KW stations. What effect do you see on the economic structure of most markets of substantial expansion in the number of available competing signals?*

A. First of all I don't think it will happen, if you're talking about the 9 kz rule. I think if it happens it will be disastrous to radio broadcasters, especially to the small market guys. It's going to cost upwards of $15-20,000 to retool your facilities. In some small markets, that's the *gross* billing.

As far as the reduction of the 50 KWs is concerned, they are a dinosaur. The reason they existed was service to the hinterlands. With the growth of radio they are a thing of the past. Their existence is really not important.

It's unfortunate that all too few of the people who make the rules for broadcasters have ever been out "in the trenches." Few of them have ever had to try and make a business out of it.

Q. *You are aware that there is an attempt at this time to develop a new "network" concept in radio. There are news networks in existence and Mutual is working on the development of a new music network which would be able to provide live concerts to radio via satellite and microwave relay with very little fidelity loss. Is there a future for the network concept and what kinds of services do you see as being provided?*

A. I think the network concept is just going to explode. I think that every service you can offer on a local basis now will be conceivable and really desirable, on a network program. The sports network is very attractive as are the concert performances. A disk jockey show might be very acceptable right now from midnight to 6:00 a.m. Let's say you've got an all-night man making $13,000/year. If the network can supply your programming for zero dollars, why not? The network can afford to hire top talent. Maybe it would be good from 8:00 p.m. to midnight. It's almost a return to the old NBC "Monitor" concept. A lot of things like that will be provided in the near future.

Q. *Do you think it's possible to see entire station programming, such as wall-to-wall music concepts, being provided as network broadcasts?*

A. Absolutely! Especially the Shulke, Bonneville, "good music" FM concept that doesn't need to be localized.

Q. *Radio stood up to the challenge of the movies. Radio grew in strength while being challenged by television. Now radio faces the challenge of in-home entertainment systems like videotape cassettes and video discs. What's radio's future in this respect? Will radio's effect on the American audience decline? Will radio find new ways to attract and hold audiences?*

A. I think videotape cassettes and video discs will have no impact on radio at all, especially on AM. I think the big challenge coming up is not to radio, but to television. Multiple signal distribution systems, satellite broadcasts from around the world—you might get a bullfight in Madrid, live, in stereo, in high fidelity pictures—pose a challenge to television.

I don't see cable as a threat to radio because it doesn't have personality, and because it isn't mobile.

Don Berns

Don Berns is a talented, multifaceted dinosaur. Like the dinosaur, he looms large, is gentle, and makes an impact wherever he appears. Like the dinosaur, he may be fading from the landscape as the species has difficulty reproducing itself.

Years of sterile, formula radio have stunted the growth of radio talents like Berns. Low radio wage scales have driven many of the best to television . . . where I think we'll see Don Berns one day.

Happily, however, somewhere out there are one or two or more kids who have the opportunity to be exposed to Don Rose in S.F.O., Gary Owens in L.A., Fred Winston in Chicago, Dan Ingram in New York—or Don Berns in Pittsburgh—and in that exposure see the possibilities.

Q. Your're one of the top personality jocks in the country, and you've worked some of the top "personality" stations in the country. Tell us about some of those stations. What I'd like to know in particular is how their station "personality" differed.

A. I consider the top "personality" stations I've worked for to be WKBW (Buffalo), KLIF (Dallas), KFMB (San Diego) and now WTAE (Pittsburgh). I'm not going to go back before WKBW because we'd be getting into '60s radio, which is a totally different bag.

Of all the stations I've mentioned, WKBW (1970-1975) was probably the best in terms of personalities because of the completely different styles of the people who were on the station, as well as the expert guidance of the man I still consider to be the most innovative and creative I have ever worked for—Jeff Kaye. When you consider that KB had such diverse personalities as Dan Neaverth (homespun/warm/funny/Buffalo born and bred), Sandy Beach (not a jock; an entertainer who is most likely the funniest, quickest person I have ever worked with on the air), Jack Armstrong (the fastest mouth in the world; not all of his bits worked, but they went by so fast you never noticed . . . and you either loved him or hated him, but you were aware of him), and me (at the time an "emerging" personality, I was rough to be sure, but had things to say, bits to do, and the freedom to do them). It's no wonder that the station was a winner, although we never did beat WBEN, the old-line MOR that totally dominated the market.

KB had a magic and a charm. Jeff guided the station in the direction of "predictable unpredictability." Just about anything could happen on the air (and off) and normally did. Good contests, not just the call-in-and-win variety, the annual Halloween extravaganza (including Jeff's own version of *War of the Worlds*), the seven-hour annual broadcast for the Salvation Army's 700 fund (yours truly broadcasting outdoors in a Santa Claus outfit in the middle of December), and the most sensational production I've ever heard. During the Bills football broadcasts Jeff was able to make a dull football club sound exciting by being creative with his production of the games. A big plus was our involvement in the local music scene. It made us unique. Each summer we would stage outdoor free "Music to the People" concerts featuring local bands and perhaps a national headliner or two. The concerts drew thousands of people.

I could go on and on about Jeff Kaye's KB but I think you get the idea. Not only was it an exciting station to work at but it was exciting to listen to. The station had a personality of its own, and within that personality each jock had a separate identity that fit within the overall framework of this non-formatted, highly visible radio station.

Next comes KLIF, which I include on the list because of Charley and Harrigan's morning show and my afternoon madness. It's where I began doing the schtick I'm doing now—one liners, off-the-wall bits, and the phasing out of "voices." The station was a cross between Top 40 and A/C but was lacking in a solid direction. When the ratings dropped severely after a major promotion in the fall of '75, it all went downhill from there.

KLIF suffered from an insurmountable image problem. The attempts to generate a station image through personalities, promotions, and music never worked. It seemed as though we were all going separate ways on the air with nothing to hold us together. KLIF was the weakest of the personality stations I worked for.

KFMB was the first adult contemporary station I worked for. Because of that, the personality of the station was considerably more adult. Emphasis was on community affairs rather than on-air contests and music.

Although Scott Burton was the PD, Bobby Rich initiated most of the promotions we did. Bobby was the PD of our highly successful Top 40 FM outlet (B-100) and did a couple of hours on KFMB every night. Bobby did a weekly feature he called the "Turkey Hour." It featured everything from the Archies singing "Sugar Sugar" to totally unknown old singles he would play accompanied with the sounds of turkeys gobbling in the background.

Bobby was the best of a lineup of good, but not outstanding, personalities. He is witty, with a good voice, and knows how to use sound effects to his advantage on the air. (A bad line might be followed by a clunking noise that set the line apart and made it funny.)

The morning team of Mac Hudson and Joe Bauer were adult—on the order of Lohman and Barclay, and more interesting than Charlie and Harrigan.

The station's promotions were community-oriented and included events like live coverage of the annual Southern California Exposition and Fair, the annual Leukemia Radiothon and live coverage of the Thunderbolt Regatta. (Picture a super-powered hydroplane race, a crowd of 100,000 people, and up there, above the crowd, a raised platform on which there are TV crews, radio reporters, and the station's call letters.)

In conclusion to your first question I would say that "personality" stations differ mainly in their approach to personality. A disk jockey does not have to be funny to be a recognized personality. Clark Anthony at KFMB is warm, personable, reads his own poetry on the air, is rarely funny, and is a highly rated personality in the market. He fits the personality of his station. If the afternoon compliments the morning, the basic framework is set. If the mid-day show somehow compliments both what precedes and what follows, a definite station sound (or personality) will be perceived by the listener. The audience knows what to expect when the station is on.

Most stations play the same music so the presentation of the music becomes crucial to "personality."

WKBW was successful because it had unpredictable predictability combined with a long-established reputation. KLIF tried to establish an overall personality but the long-established rock and roll reputation of the call letters precluded any success. KFMB was minimally successful because they vacillated. Since I left they picked up Padres baseball and it complimented their image . . . and it worked.

WTAE has the same success story. The Pittsburgh Steelers get us ratings. The station's personality keeps the listeners. It's still a battle against the old line leader KDKA but our better-defined personality scores well with the 18-34 demographic.

Although most of the personality stations in the country are A/C I have noticed the infusion of more personality into Top 40 lately and it comes like a breath of fresh air.

Q. *The word "personality" has been kicked around quite a bit. I've heard stations described as personality which were, to my ear, mechanical, formula formats. Define "personality" as you see it.*

A. As I see it, a *personality* is someone who has something to say. It doesn't matter if the person is funny, as long as something halfway intelligent is said. If the jock rambles, it's the job of a good PD to steer him in the right direction. The mechanical radio of the past few years has produced a scarcity of personality jocks.

A lot of PDs are blowing smoke when they describe their stations as "personality" when all they have their jocks doing are mechanical presentations with an occasional "Shotgun Sam Boogie Down" thrown in. These stations aren't personality; they are gross distortions of what the concept of radio as a communications medium should be about. The kids coming along had only these time/temperature jocks to emulate. The idea of what personality is evolved into what a personality *isn't*. Good A/C stations turned that around. People starting in the business today have some real personalities to listen to.

One of the sad things about radio is that the training ground for young jocks could be college radio but they are no longer teaching the important things. On my last visit to WBRU (Providence-Brown Univ.) I talked with a girl whose life's desire is to be an AOR jock. She had no concept of any other kind of radio. She didn't know anything about demographics. She didn't know personalities from other stations, nor did she know anything about any other format than AOR. Whatever happened to those long nights in the dorm, or the college radio station, tuning in New York to hear what Cousin Brucie was doing on WABC, or trying to catch the first few minutes of Claven and Finch before sunrise pattern change? All these kids know today is who is on WBCN (Boston) or WNEW-FM (New York). The basics have been lost and it's a disappointment.

Q. *The most common error made by jocks attempting the personality approach is what is known as "running off at the mouth"—too much talk, too little content. Where does "personality" end and "too much talk" begin?*

A. That's the job of the PD. He decides where "too much talk too little content" begins. If the PD can't discipline his jocks into shaping an overall station sound, he isn't doing his job. However, if you've got the bucks to hire good personalities who know their acts, there shouldn't be much pruning necessary. New kids with talent and signs of greatness should be nurtured. That was one of Jeff Kaye's talents and achievements, and I'll always be thankful to him for what he did for me.

Q. *Who in your opinion were, or are, some of the great radio per-*

sonalities? Did any of them influence you?

A. I was influenced by a lot of great radio personalities. My early days in radio were spent as carbon copies of Joey Reynolds (WKBW-WDRC), Ken Griffin (WPOP) and Sandy Beach (WDRC), all of whom worked in Hartford when I was a youth. I didn't know what radio was but I knew those people could make me laugh. These guys are the Holy Trinity in my opinion though there are others I consider great. From the old WDRC-WPOP days I would put Ron Landry at the top. My friends and I used to discuss the silly bits he did when I was in junior high school. In the late '60s I started listening critically and got off on Dale Dorman, J.J. Jeffries, and Chuck Knapp at WRKO (Boston) and Claven and Finch and Dan Ingram (WABC) in New York. When I moved to Buffalo I had a chance to listen to and respect Jack Armstrong, Dan Neaverth, Pat Reilly (a man of 1000 good voices, wasted all-nights on KB because of company politics) and Casey Piotrowski. In Toronto, CHUM had a great lineup in the early '70s that included Terry Steele and Scott Carpenter. They were two of the best format jocks I've ever heard. Jungle Jay Nelson was there and he was one of the funniest. John Rhode should be included here too, because although he wasn't funny he was one of the most intelligent and interesting radio personalities I've ever heard. I'd be remiss if I didn't enter the name of Dick Smyth here in another area of radio personality. Dick was CHUM's news director and perhaps the best newsman I've ever heard. His 7:10 and 8:10 commentaries were works of art and his newscasts interesting. He had one of the best writing styles in the business. David Marsden (then at CHUM-FM and now PD at CFNY-FM Toronto) was a personality who stands out as elevating AOR personality to a height I've yet to hear anybody else reach. His nightly "let's-reach-in-the-brown-paper-bag-and-see-what-we-have" feature was a classic.

I can't think of anybody in Dallas who influenced me although Ron Chapman at KVIL is the essence of what the hometown-oriented jock should be. In San Diego I respected Hudson and Bauer and Clark Anthony at KFMB, although I would not say they influenced me. During that time KGB-FM had an all-night jock named Adrian Bolt whose laid-back style and music mixes gave that AOR outlet some class. I've already mentioned Bobby Rich and his contribution. In Los Angeles I was impressed by Lohman and Barclay and Gary Owens (KMPC). Gary influenced my current style greatly.

I'm sorry to say that I found people like the Real Don Steele and Larry Lujack disappointing. I've not found them to be vital, creative personalities—yet they have reputations for being so.

Allison Steele, WNEW-FM's "Nightbird" has impressed me. I think she's one of the best AOR jocks and certainly the best female on the air. Dick Summers (WBZ-Boston and WNEW-New York), read his own poetry on the air and was a unique personality.

Last, and not least, there was Jerry Hubeny (aka Stevens) at WICE-Providence, who got me into the business. He was only a part-timer and has since gotten out of the business but he proved that you don't have to have a great voice to have a good show. He was one of the most natural, friendly sounding jocks I've known and his friendship and sound advice will always stay with me.

Q. *Is personality radio dying? Is the market for a true personality jock like yourself shrinking, and what do you do about it?*

A. The market for true radio personalities is not dead, nor will it ever be. However, the true personalities are few because formula radio of the '60s stifled the growth of personality. There are some good jocks around who are being restricted by shortsighted formats and/or program directors. To them I say: hang in, do as much "schtick" as your format will allow, and listen to all the radio you can. When you discover a station that does the kind of radio you want to do, work toward getting there. If the format you're working doesn't allow you the freedom to create, do a tape in the production room that shows what you can do. First and foremost, stick it out. The only big money and true creativity in this business lies with the personality jock.

Q. *Given the growth of consulted formats and formula radio, where are the new personality performers to come from? Is Don Berns one of the last of a dying breed? If you were a young jock who wanted to develop a personal performance, where would you look for a job?*

A. I think the new personality performers are in the small markets and the more they listen to and emulate the personality jocks they like, the more they will develop their own personalities. I don't consider myself a dying breed because everything I say on the air is reaching some young man or woman and affecting him/her. There are only so many things that can be done on radios. Let people you admire show you the way, and then use your own creativity to build on that base.

Obviously you can't travel around the country listening to radio stations looking for a station you want to work for. You can, however, follow radio classified ads closely and look for PDs who are looking for people who do personality.

Getting close to the radio people in your market is another excellent way to look for a job. Word of mouth travels and recommendations count. I got the job I have now at WTAE on just that kind of recommendation.

Q. *What is the essence of your particular air personality? What is it that you do that you feel is different from other air personalities?*

A. I'm not sure how to describe my air personality. I'm silly, funny, warm, topical, conversational, and "relatable." It took me years to build to the point where I was comfortable with myself. It takes awareness of the news, the city, the target audience's interests, and a knowledge of how to relate to them to make it work.

The first rule in trying to be funny is editing. It's easy to overdo it. If you don't think a bit is *great,* perhaps you should leave it out. Editing also plays a part in *how* you say what you say. There's nothing worse than a jock rambling on, not making a point. Know the punchline, and know how to get there.

Above all, I try to be a pro. I take pride in what I do. That's how I feel about myself, and it's the best advice I can give.

Q. *Some performers claim that when they are behind the mike they perform to a "person." They picture someone as being on the other side of the mike and talk to him or her. Do you work that way?*

A. I work the audience, rather than a "person." At WKBW I had an engineer on the other side of the glass and he acted as an audience for me. I could get an immediate reaction. I'm a ham. I enjoy performing before people. Acting and directing are hobbies of mine and when I'm not on the air I'm often appearing in local stage productions. I try to relate to the whole audience as a person, searching for the element that will entertain the majority.

Q. *I've observed that many performers work best when they play off the audience. You've worked a lot of different areas of the country. Did your audience in Buffalo differ from the audience in San Diego, Kansas City or Pittsburgh? How did you adjust your performance?*

A. I think I learned the hard way that audiences *do* differ around the country. My particular brand of humor did not go over particularly well in Dallas, San Diego, or Kansas City. Callout research in San Diego indicated to our station "analyst" that I was abrasive. My show was very successful in Buffalo and is very strong here in Pittsburgh which gives credability to the thought that my approach fits best into a blue-collar, industrialized environment.

As to the question of adjusting my performance, I would say that working with different PDs and the transition from a Top 40 jock to A/C had more to do with adjustment than anything else. I tried to edit out elements PDs found objectionable, deferring in most cases to what I felt was their more precise understanding of the market. There have been times when I disagreed with my PD but made the adjustment anyway, knowing that the discipline I'd impose upon myself in so doing would itself contribute to my development.

For example, I used to do lots of voices. In Dallas they asked me to take them out. In San Diego I put them back in until Scott Burton told me that I sounded better than any of my voices. Then I understood that his criticism might be valid and it was my ego, not my objective evaluation, that kept fighting to bring the voices back. Freed of the voices, I began working on *me* as a personality. I developed new bits and new methods of getting those bits across.

In the long run, this development, coupled with getting a few years older and getting fired a couple of times, matured me. I still feel that I can grow—and I never want to lose that feeling—but I know that my air sound is professional and more polished and that it gets more so with every performance.

Q. *Personality radio sometimes inspires some pretty nutty telephone calls. Have you any anecdotes about crazy callers?*

A. As you know, my act doesn't include telephone callers on the air so most of my "nutty" callers have been off-air comments on something I've said. I have done some phone-oriented bits, however. Once I had listeners call in the dumb joke of the day. Another time we searched for the "class" act" of the day. The idea here was to look for some silly thing that happened during the day to one of the audience that was beyond the realm of sanity. We all do silly things every day, like leaving the bag of groceries on the roof of the car and then driving off, and we'd ask the audience to tell us about them. Of course there are the usual phone calls from groupies or propositions of one sort or another, but in radio those hardly classify as unusual.

Q. *You are working in Pittsburgh now, at WTAE. What's unique about Pittsburgh? What makes the city easy—or difficult—to play to?*

A. Pittsburgh is a very easy city to work to. Disk jockeys have always been held in esteem here. They've been listened to; the city has had its share of personality jocks and the people have an appreciation for this kind of radio.

The number one common denominator is sports. The Pirates, Steelers, and Pitt Panthers are talked about everywhere. You hear sports talk on the streets, in restaurants, and at the ballet. Keep your ears open and somebody is talking about sports. My favorite Pittsburgh sports story actually happened to me. I had come into town for a job interview and was standing at the airline counter picking up my return flight ticket when a guy tapped me on the shoulder and said "Did you hear what Myron Cope said tonight?" The town is so sports-oriented that he immediately assumed I'd know Myron Cope was the sports commentator and color analyst for the Steelers. I don't suppose it ever occurred to him that someone in Pittsburgh would not know Myron Cope.

Another nice thing here in the Steel City is that people are very music-oriented. Music trivia is a hobby of mine and provides me with an avenue to relate to a music interested audience.

The biggest problem with Pittsburgh is its provincialism. A lot of old East Coast ethnic and religious based customs make it difficult to relate to the new and the hip. Chic is not necessarily in. On the positive side, the simplistic lifestyle makes relating to the people easier.

Q. *Inflation is rampant, unemployment is reaching record highs, word tensions are heating up and a Presidential commission reports that unless substantial changes are made in the way we live, there will be mass starvation in the year 2000. What's funny today? What are people laughing at?*

A. People laugh at what they've always laughed at—themselves. I usually stay away from sensitive areas like the economy, politics, and the world situation. I make jokes about sports, television, movies, holidays, leisure time activities, roads and potholes and such. I comb newspapers, magazines, and wire copy for "off the wall" material. Material that relates to humans as humans is what people are laughing at.

Q. *Comedy of today seems to be dominated by the zanies. Steve Martin, one of the hottest comics of the day, uses comedy that is a throwback to Three Stooges slapstick. The cerebral comic, the social and political satirist seems to be missing from the scene. What happened? Has it affected your comedy?*

A. I've already discussed part of the answer to this question. However I would say that my comedy has been affected by the zaniness of the type of comedy that has mass appeal today. People don't seem to want intelligent comedy today. Satire and cynicism force them to dwell on negative influences and they reject that. Satire doesn't work well on radio appealing to mass audience, as it encourages negativism among those who understand what you're talking about and goes over the heads of the others.

You have to know your audience. If they want silliness, give it to them. If you can work in a message, all the better. If you are seeking to entertain, you've got to leave out the negative influences and negative situations.

Q. *The rule of thumb in radio has always been that it takes an hour of preparation for every hour of program. How much preparation do you find you have to do for your show? Is much of your stuff spontaneous?*

A. There has only been one period in my life where I did any concentrated preparation. That was when I did mornings in Kansas City. I found it necessary to come in early to study the newspaper. Otherwise, my show prep consists of pulling as much music as possible and preparing the commercial schedule in advance. (No traffic department in the country seems to understand spot balance, and clumsily scheduled spots can ruin a good show.) Everything I do on the air with the exception of an occasional pretaped bit is extemporaneous. After 14 years on the air, there is a sort of "mental format" which sorts things out and organizes patterns I can follow during the show. It has been my experience that just as a fighter can overtrain for a fight and fight after he's passed his peak of training, a disk jockey can prepare so well that he loses the spark of spontaneity on the air.

Q. *You do a lot of acting in community theater. You've also recorded an album as a singer. Do you feel this experience has been helpful to your on air performance and do you recommend it as a training for jocks?*

A. Yes, of course! Acting has not only been a creative outlet and hobby for me but has been extremely helpful to my radio career. The act of performing in front of live audience has given me valuable experience as an MC, in discipline, and in comedic timing. Taking direction on stage is related to taking direction from a PD. Comedy timing is definitely related to delivering lines on the radio. People you meet in community theater represent a cross-section of the audience. They all work regular jobs, have families and problems which often act as thought starters for material on my show. Getting out among the audience is often a prerequisite for outside station promotion and in theater you do it, and you enjoy it at the same time.

My experience in the recording studio gives me a knowledge of production techniques, arrangements, mike technique, and musical values. You don't need these things to play records, but you need them to understand records and music. I recorded my album in Buffalo. I learned a lot about Buffalo from the musicians I met and worked with. That information reflected in my on-air performance. The album enhanced my reputation. The sum total improved my program.

Q. You've been music director for many of the stations you've worked. Do you believe in music research? What kind? Do you do much of it? Do you trust your ear to pick music your audience will like?

A. Music is an area in which I am outspoken. I don't claim any special knowledge of music research techniques or a complete understanding of passive research information analysis.

My first MD job was at WKBW. There and at WYSL our criteria was sales and how the record sounded to our ears. By the time I became an MD again (at WHB-Kansas City), passive research was in. I believe in the basic premise of passive research but I temper it with a human factor, sales information, and request action.

If you believe in passive research, I think the information gained can be important to knowing when to add a song and what rotation to give it. High negatives among your target audience would seem to indicate a pretty good reason not to play it regardless of sales figures or national chart action. Some records have highly regional appeal which give them big sales but limited appeal in certain geographic areas. Passive research gives particular attention to negative responses rather than positive ones. Positive influences might include such things as acceptance in your market by other stations, positive reaction on passive callouts, artist, or sound images which fit your station.

Music direction solely on the basis of research leaves out human factors which could be very strong and represent a major element in doing the music director's job.

Yes, I do trust my ear to pick hits. I've been in this business a long time and I can hear some of them. Those I can't hear, I wait on and study the information as it develops. I love music. I collect records. I often take a piece of music I'm considering home and live with it for a while before I make a final decision. It's exciting to pick a record and then see it through to become a hit. It's one of the few tangible rewards we get. I value the gold and platinum record awards I've won very much.

Q. You read a lot about people dropping "teen" records in order to attract "adult" listeners. Yet the music on most of the stations seems to show very little variation. Is there such a thing as a "teen" record, or is a hit a hit, with appeal to a broad base?

A. I don't believe that a hit is a hit. Yes, you can hear virtually the same music on all stations. It's what you *don't* hear that makes the difference. There are some records which are definitely turnoffs for adults. Fractionalization of the market has created subtle differences between stations, giving the audience a wider choice and developing definite station music images.

Q. One of my favorite music programmers, Rick Sklar (WABC) once said something to me to the effect that any record which becomes a solid hit got enough airplay to become familiar to the adult listener. Consequently, a record that was a "teen" record today would be an "adult" record five or six weeks down the line if it became an honest hit. It was part of the rationale for the

WABC music policy of the time of seeming to be late on some hit records. During that period WABC was the number one station in the number 1 market in the world. The formula obviously worked for him. What do you think about that? Do you agree or disagree?

A. I agree that waiting on a particular record may be beneficial to a station looking to appeal to the adult listener. This is especially true if you're using passive research techniques to verify audience appeal of the music. If a record is in doubt, I wait. There is plenty of product available to fill the void. I've seen records start out quickly with younger audiences, go on to attract request action from adults and develop tremendous negatives as the burnout factor developed. If you hold back and then determine that you were wrong, you're all that much more certain when you *do* make the add that you've added a hit.

Q. *Where does Don Berns go from here? If "personality" radio fades and formula radio dominates the air, will you change your act? Do you feel there will always be a market, somewhere, for a true personality?*

A. Yes, I feel that there will always be a market for a true radio personality, even if it's only in the highly coveted morning drive show. I feel that personality is on its way back, especially in the adult contemporary stations that deal primarily with the 25-44 audience. These people are my peers. As long as I can relate to and entertain them, I will be valuable as a radio personality. Everybody is not for my act, and my act isn't for everybody.

At the moment, I'm concentrating on settling down in Pittsburgh. I plan to stay here as long as they'll have me.

Q. *You've responded to some prepared questions. Now, I'd like to give you a chance to fill in whatever blanks we left. Are there any comments you'd like to make, any words of wisdom you'd like to pass along to our readers about radio, personality, or anything else?*

A. There are a couple of things I would like to add. I'd like to talk to those people who want to get into radio comedy. There are a lot of people who poo-poo comedy services. I'm not one of them, but I think it's important to pick and choose the services you use, and to use them wisely.

First, do you have a sense of humor? If you sat down and tried to write your own material, how would it sound? How would you present it? When you look at a comedy service, look for one that presents material that would sound like something you'd write. Otherwise, the comedy would distort your personality. My first rule is to buy material that sounds like something I might have written for myself.

Second, comedy should never be presented on the air in willy-nilly fashion. Just like a music format, comedy needs a rhythm, a rhyme, and a reason. You'll come across many lines that can't be presented out of context and there is no easy way to set them up. When I reach that situation, I usually begin to set the line up early by saying something like "Later this hour I'll tell you about" or "the radio program that notes", etc. For my show, comedy needs a format. There has to be a place for it—or you've got to create the place for it.

I use a lot of topical material and that too needs set up. One good place to put in topical lines is over the record intro out of the newscast. The line usually relates to something in the cast, provides topical comedy, and at the same time it makes the point that the news is interesting and valuable to listen to.

I use some continuing bits. I tie one of them in with the weather forecast. It's the "On This Day in History" line and may relate to astrological forecasts, TV previews, etc. I try to limit these to no more than two per hour.

One source for material is the wire service. They usually print a lot of "kicker" stories and those the news department doesn't use I rip off for my show.

Extended bits can be useful. Some areas for this kind of bit are phony commercials, dos and don'ts, the radio soap opera of the air, New Years predictions, etc. If we don't have a contest formatted, I try to work in one of these bits. However, one bit per hour is maximum.

The thing to remember most about comedy is that you can overdo it. Don't try to be funny every time you open your mouth. Editing is extremely important. Every line won't work, but even your best line can be buried in too much material.

I use a lot of outside material. Some of the sources are:

☐ *Current Comedy:* A monthly service out of Dallas. Great for topical lines and "on this day in history" bits.
☐ *O'Bits:* Dan O'Day's off-the-wall humor develops some excellent extended bits.
☐ *Hype, Ink:* This used to be my best service for extended bits. Since I found O'Bits, I use Hype as filler material.
☐ *Orben's Current Comedy:* It's limited in scope, but good for topical comedy. I've used it for the past nine years.
☐ *O'Liners:* Good filler stuff, from Dan O'Day.
☐ *The Electric Weenie:* The best for cross-plugging zingers and TV previews. I re-write much of the Weenie material to customize it to my delivery.

In using service material, don't hesitate to rewrite it if you like the punchline but have difficulty with the approach.

It costs money to buy comedy services but I find the expense worthwhile and tax deductable. I keep all of the material in a file, cross-indexed and updated for handy reference.

That's about it, except for my recommendations for people wanting to get into radio: Stay away from most "broadcasting schools," which are primarily ripoffs. The best way of learning the business is experience, and the best experience I can recommend is a college radio station. That way you can learn the ins and outs of all parts of the business and find out whether it's right for you and you're right for it. In the meantime you're getting a college education, which means that if you decide you don't want a career in radio, or it doesn't want you, you've got something to fall back on. I went to Brown University and learned a great deal about this business just by keeping my eyes and ears open around the station and eventually I landed a part time job on a Providence Top 40 outlet.

Above all, if you really believe in what you do, keep at it. Desire is the best way to achieve success. Humility and objectivity must not be overlooked as prime assets to taking a career to its limits.

Gene Taylor

I first heard of Gene Taylor when he was with WLS-radio, the 50,000 watt clear channel giant in Chicago. It was years later, in Newport Beach, California when I met him. Gene was involved with a friend of mine in the operation of what I dismissed as a typical ripoff broadcast school at KEZY in Anaheim. To my genuine surprise and delight I found that Gene Taylor had a real desire to teach, a talent for doing it, and an inherent honesty that translated into legitimate education for his students. At that point Gene Taylor turned me from an admirer into a fan.

I think you will find his candid responses to my questions typical of the man I am proud to call my friend.

Q. *For those readers who may not be familiar with the name Gene Taylor, will you give us some idea of your background in radio?*

A. One way or the other, I've been messing around in radio since 1948. I went the usual route of small midwestern towns; after a couple of years of that, I got back to my hometown of Minneapolis and settled in there for several years at a couple of the smaller stations.

I moved to Milwaukee in 1958 and did a couple of years for Bartell radio as "Happy O'Day." (Can you believe that?) In Chicago in 1960 I was a jock at WLS when they made the switch from "The Prairie Farmer" to the "Silver Dollar Survey" station. I worked under Ralph Beaudine and Sam Holman till Sam headed into N.Y. for his abortive stay at WABC. Beaudine bumped me up to PD at that time and that seems to have been the beginning of the good times and the learning radio. I became GM at WLS in 1966 and stayed at that until the end of '71 when I went into Cleveland for the Globetrotters to GM WIXY and WDOK. Thank God they fired me after a year! Cleveland is the butt of the Earth. I hit California in '73, owned an art gallery for a year or so and then got into the teaching business.

Q. *For several years now you've been operating a broadcast school in connection with KEZY radio in Anaheim, California. What would you say is the most common misconception about radio that your students have when they first come to your school?*

A. The biggest problem I run into with the kids is the simple fact that they've gotten to know radio in Southern California and presume it's like that all over the world. From the sound of their favorite music stations, they presume that all they have to do is get a year's experience and then come back to L.A. and sound like the jocks on KMET, KLOS or KEZY . . . you know, laid back and sloppy. They simply will not admit that they might have to go out and do some real dues-paying.

Q. *Obviously not everybody who graduates from broadcast school is headed for an on-the-air job. However, broadcast education can lead to fulfilling jobs in radio in other areas. I know you stress this point in your school. Will you discuss some of those other areas of broadcast for us and what the young broadcaster can look forward to in them?*

A. The biggest thing that kids can do about getting into radio is be willing to take *anything*! If a sales gig opens up, take it! Part-time air work, production, writing, *anything* to get to a station and be there in case something happens. They've got to equip themselves with as many skills as is humanly possible—typing, writing, production, editing—in other words, moxie!

Q. *It's understandable that some students would come to your school with an idea that radio is a glamorous business in which everybody makes big money and enjoys a "star" status. Speaking in terms of today, what can the broadcast school graduate realistically expect to find as a starter job in terms of market size and salary range?*

A. Starter gigs are going between $550 and $700 (per month), strictly depending on the market and station. Market size will range from 5000 to 25,000. If a kid is willing to go anywhere, he'll get himself started. Whether or not he goes from there, that's up to him/her.

Q. *When you interview prospective students for your school, what qualities do you look for? What makes you accept a student for the school?*

A. I look to see if they can afford it, I really do listen to the voice and the reading ability and, if possible, look for a kid who's got a little guts. There is not a thing wrong with having an ego, as long as he knows how to use it.

Q. *In the interview situation I know that you often have to suggest to prospective students that a broadcast career may not be for them. What might you see in a candidate that would make you turn them down for acceptance into your program?*

A. The biggest single problem for me—or anybody in the radio school thing—is simply that *kids can't read*. That's it! You know as well as I do that you can work with a person's voice, but if they can't get the words off the page, they're dead.

Q. *I know that the course of study you offer at the KEZY school covers a wide spectrum of areas the student will encounter in radio station life. Discuss for us some of the areas you cover in your school.*

A. Major areas are voice work and equipment handling. I do try to give them programming, sales, some technical (enough to get a third), writing (commercials only), D.J. techniques, a tad of traffic (enough so they know what it is); in short, a bit of everything that goes on at a radio station.

Q. As a responsible broadcaster I know that you have expressed concern about some of the broadcast schools operating around the country who may not be delivering a quality education in the field. What kinds of questions should the student evaluating a broadcast course ask about the school to assure that the preparation he/she is receiving is relevant?

A. The only thing the student should concern himself with are who teaches and what is the placement percentage. Do kids *really* get gigs after the course is over.

Q. Do you have any words of advice or caution, you'd like to pass on to young broadcasters or potential broadcasters?

A. Be willing to starve for a couple of years. Be willing to work 20 hours a day if that's what it takes to get and keep the job. Be willing to go anywhere that will pay you a couple of bucks more and give you the chance to learn something new about the business.

Terry Young

Terry Young (not his real name) is what he has always wanted to be—a star on the radio—and in today's radio that is not an easy task.

Terry Young grew up listening to radio when being in radio made you a star. The fact of your being there lent an aura to your person. He entered radio at a time when most of the gloss was gone and the mystery faded. His performance and his personality hark back to a time past, when being on the radio was important and being on the radio made you important. The odds were against him and he should have failed at this self-pronounced goal of becoming a star. But he didn't.

At WLEE, Terry Young was on the radio from 7 to midnight on a 5000 watt directional signal that was fast fading in its ability to influence the market. We were keeping the radio station alive with promotion, programming tricks, and energy. We were beating a 20,000 watt stereo competitor because we willed it so and part of the "magic" of radio is that the will to win is the key ingredient to winning.

In that atmosphere, Terry Young became a star. You liked him or you hated him, but I think it's safe to say that nobody interested in radio in Richmond could ignore him. He was what he wanted to be—a star—when it wasn't fashionable to be one.

Q. You broke into radio at a rather young age. What made you want to be a disk jockey? Do you remember your first feelings on the matter?

A. The Beatles—hearing the disk jockey play Beatles records. Liking the Beatles made me feel "in." I wanted to grow my hair long and be the disk jockey who played the Beatles.

Q. Do you have any heroes in the business? Are there any disk jockeys you particularly admire and who have influenced you?

A. Tom T. Hall was the first disk jockey to ever influence me because he was the first disk jockey who didn't say "go away kid, you bother me." Tom T. Hall let me cue up my first record and sit behind the control board when I was 11 years old. He was a DJ on a little country station. The first time I wanted to be a jock was when I was 11.

Jack Armstrong was my number one "hero." I first heard of him in 1966. I was a jingle freak, I used to tape all the jingle packages. You could hear all the radio stations at night. I got all set up to tape the Jim Labarbara show—he would play a record, a jingle, and then talk. Then a record, a jingle, and a record. You could get the whole jingle package within an hour.

I got set up to tape the jingle package and there was this guy on the air named Jack Armstrong and he was really crazy. He talked all over the records, he had drop-ins and sound effects and he was very funny. I used to try to copy him. I thought he was great.

Buzz Bennett was a hero of mine. Even though he only had two rating books in every town, his radio was very hip. He was better than WABC. His form of radio was the kind of radio I wanted to do. The way he did his promos, the way he did his music, the way his jocks came across on the air was 1980ish. Buzz Bennett was a genius. Bob Paiva influenced me more to treat radio as show business than anybody I've ever met. The main thing he said to me was "You want to make 50 people go crazy about you, go over and shake hands with that kid. Tell him who you are, and he'll tell 50 of his friends." I thought, "I can't do that . . . I'm too shy." But I did it, and the kid went off and told his friends that he'd just met Terry Young. It works! Radio is show business. You (Bob) made WLEE the most visible radio station in Richmond, and for an AM station, we killed them. I'll work for you again!

Q. *How did you break into the business. How did you get your first job?*

A. My dad was in the business. He bought a daytime rock station in Richmond, Virginia, and he switched it to country. I was 14 years old and had a third class ticket. All his jocks quit, so I had to segue records. I wasn't allowed to talk. In February 1971 I went to work at WTVR Richmond as a rock jock. I worked weekends . . . and was a senior in high school. After that I went into the Air Force for six months, and then went to WRNC in Raleigh, North Carolina. I was in 7 to midnight against Rick Dees and Mike Mitchell. Dees did 10-2, Mike Mitchell did 6-10. I did 7-midnight and I kicked their butts. I had a 41 in teens; they had an 11. They were playing the Carpenters and I was playing the Stones. I whipped their butts and went from there to WROV in Roanoke. Then I went to WKAZ in Charleston, West Virginia, to do 7-midnight. That's when I met you when you were in a "Dunk the Jock" booth at a fair. It was another visible WLEE stunt. I came to work for you in 1973. Richmond was my hometown; I went to school there.

Q. *What was it like being on the radio in your hometown?*

It was dynamite. I worked for a number-one radio station that had a trailer and remote studios and could play ball. It was dynamite to work 7-midnight at WLEE and be number one.

Q. *When you worked at WLEE in the 7-midnight slot, you developed a* very high-energy performance. In fact you were known as a "screamer." Can you describe the technique you used to develop and maintain this high-energy style?

A. There's nothing to it. You just act excited. I was into screaming on the radio as an attention-getter. The reason the Rolling Stones record "Emotional Rescue" was a hit with the kids is because Mick Jagger uses a really strange, high-sounding voice at the beginning of the song. The kids can relate to strange things. If it's strange, it's cool. Not only was I a screamer, I was a *strange* screamer. I've always believed in being very mysterious about yourself on that radio.

Q. *I know that your high-energy style was considered by some of your friends to be a "teeney-bopper" style and they encouraged you to slow down your pace and be more "FM." How did you handle the conflict between your personal life and your radio performance when you received such criticism from your friends?*

A. Well, I started slowing down but the main change that I made was that when I opened my mouth I didn't make an ass of myself.

We had a situation recently when it was 101 degrees. Some of the schools had to let the kids out because they didn't have air conditioning. The kids who were in schools without air conditioning who didn't get the day off went on strike. On the air I talked about that situation and related directly to the audience.

I used to do a long sign-off. I'm no longer allowed to do that but the last thing I do on the air is to say "See you later, Debbie Slater." Debbie Slater was a person in my life. Every day on the radio I say "See you later, Debbie Slater." You have no idea how many girls come up to me and ask "Who is Debbie Slater?" Or I'll ask somebody for a date and they'll want to know if Debbie Slater will object. It adds to being mysterious. You've got to be mysterious.

Q. *One of the elements of your success in Richmond was your ability to appeal to a "crossover" audience. For the first time in Richmond radio history, a radio station attracted not only a substantial portion of the white audience but was able to show very substantial black audience as well. What did you do, what kind of approach, did you use to attract this "crossover" audience? Was it the kind of music you played? Was it your approach? Or was it a bit of both?*

A. When I left Charleston, West Virginia, to go to work for WLEE the most requested records were "Uneasy Rider" by Charlie Daniels and "Ramblin' Man" by the Allman Brothers. Those were the songs they were asking for. Those were the ones I played. When I moved to Richmond the most requested song was "Jungle Boogie" by Kool and the Gang. A lot of other black songs were requested. I can remember "Let's Get It On" by Marvin Gaye. That's what they asked for. You've got to be visible with blacks. We pulled the WLEE mobile studio up the school at lunch hour; we'd take the three hottest black songs, and we'd play the same songs over and over. The kids would stick their heads out, see us, get a good impression and go back to class. You walk through a city park in New York and the black kids aren't listeing to WPLJ. They're listening to WKTU and WBLS. When you're in a market with a lot of blacks—and New Orleans is 63% black—you play black songs, play them out of the box. We added Stevie Wonder out of the box. We added Donna Summer out of the box. We added Earth, Wind and Fire out of the box. We were the first station to play Queen's "Another One Bites the Dust" or Diana Ross's "Upside Down" or "I'm Coming Out" or the S.O.S. band record. Those are the records that win you the audience. The phones go bananas.

In 1973 we added the Doobie Brothers' "Long Train Running" and Paul McCartney's "My Love Does it Good" out of the box. The phones went crazy. Now it's 1980; we add the new Doobie Brothers out of the box and we add the new Paul McCartney record out of the box and we get no requests. The phones are dead on those songs. But we add the S.O.S. band and we get instant reaction.

Damn Vanilla PDs program to their own lifestyles, or the audience they *want* to attract, and never get out on the screen to see who's listening to the radio and who's watching the video cassettes. I went to a white party and people were sitting around watching a movie on video cassette. I left and walking down Canal Street I ran into a black kid carrying a radio, listening to "Another One Bites the Dust" on my station—enjoying it. I rest my case.

Q. *Another important element of your success in Richmond was your availability for outside appearances. I think you appeared in more places, at more schools, and did more remotes than anybody had ever done in Richmond before. Can you tell us something about these appearances and what you feel you gained from them and why they worked for you?*

A. The most visible radio station is the most listened-to radio station. You taught me that and I'll never forget it. Anytime I can go to an old folks' home, to a school, to *anywhere*. I *go*. Tomorrow I'm pulling my car up (I drive a station car—a VW that says "B-Buggie, Terry Young" on the side) to a water slide. It's a huge slide that attracts a lot of people. I'll pull up, give out some bumper stickers, records, or whatever, and I'll slide with the kids. I never, *never* let them know about my life. I act mysterious as possible, but still warm. Make as many appearances as possible. Go to yard sales, block parties—do *anything*. Get out and shake hands. A disk jockey must be a politician to the people.

Q. *Since leaving WLEE you've had an opportunity to work a different town and two different stations, as well as a different time slot. Describe the changes you've had to make in your performance to adapt to the different time slot and the different audiences.*

A. I always play a lot of rock and roll along with black music. I have always attracted a large number of male listeners because I do concentrate on some rock and roll. When I moved to New Orleans to work at WTIX I did 7-midnight and had a 7.9 in men. I beat the FMs in men 18-plus. With those numbers they moved me to afternoons and told me to slow down. I moved and didn't slow down. I did my act. The men were there; we kicked butt. I

133

lasted through eight books at WTIX. By the time the eighth book was over they had me so slowed down, so toned out, that all I could play was "Still" by the Commodores and "Rise" by Herb Alpert. It was ridiculous for me to work at that station. B-97 opened up and offered me afternoon drive, music director, $400 a week plus remote talent—and that's serious money, $150 an appearance—it's a killer. I came over here and worked my butt off. I worked 14 hours a day. We put the format on the air and shot from a 4.3 to a 10.3 in one book. WTIX is no longer the number one radio station.

    Q. *Looking back from this vantage point, was it worth it? Would you do it again? If you would, what changes would you make?*

    A. Yes, I would do it again. Yes, it was worth it. But I would think three times about doing something (instead of twice) before I do it.

    Q. *Where does Terry Young go from here? Is there something you'd like to do? Where do you see yourself years from now?*

    A. I have a nightclub act now. It's called Terry Young "get crazy" night. In New Orleans you can get a drink anywhere. I just get them drunk. I tell them jokes, crazy one-liners. People get attracted because their friends are there, and when so many of their friends are there I don't have to work as hard. I do "Get Crazy" night every Thursday night from 11 p.m. to 2:30 in the morning, and we pack 900 people into this club. I get $150—it's another way to make your living. Ten years from now I see myself on the Johnny Carson show, doing standup comedy, or hosting *Family Feud*. Doing crazy night and getting audiences involved in my show has made me convinced that I've got the talent to get on television. I don't know how I'm going to do it, but I'm going to do it. Television is next for Terry Young.

    Programming? They only want you when you're hot. You cannot be a program director, concentrating on the radio station, and be a star jock. You've got to be one or the other. Right now I have a great PD; I'm the music director and I'm a star on the radio and that's what I want to do.

    Q. *When young people interested in radio ask you how to get into the business, what do you tell them?*

    A. "Bust your butt." Put yourself into everything you do like your life depended on it. Take care of every little detail, and pull it off. Run with the flow. Observe others. Know their weaknesses. Know your own weaknesses. Be mysterious. Be a nice guy; be a warm guy. The guy who makes it in the '80s is the guy the people want to hug. They have to love you. When they hug you, you're there.

Clark Smidt

    My association with this marvelous young broadcaster dates back to the time when I was music director of WPOP in Hartford and Clark was just entering the University of Hartford. As you will learn in our talk, Clark Smidt was almost singularly responsible for the building and operation of WWUH Radio at the University of Hartford and in performing that task became a major contributor to the development of college radio during a period of time when that entity flourished.

Clark has since gone on to become an influential broadcaster in the Boston market and the creator of one of the more successful "mellow rock" formats.

I think you will find my talk with him informative, interesting, and inspiring.

Q. *We hear lots of stories about people who got started from the "ground up." In your case, that was literally true. As I remember, you built your own station at the University of Hartford. It might interest our readers to know how you got the University to agree to the idea, and then got them to act on it.*

A. I got my first job in radio at WBIS in Bristol, Connecticut, in July of 1966 between high school and college. My family has a cottage in Litchfield, and I was going to attend the University of Hartford. From day one at the University—at the freshman orientation—I started to agitate for a radio station. I applied to four schools around New England. The others all had stations and U of H did not. When I asked about it, I was told that people had thought about it before but nobody had ever followed through on it. There was an open frequency (91.3) and WTIC in Hartford had even agreed to donate an FM transmitter. A 1000-watt transmitter was available. I ran all over the school drumming up support and at the close of my freshman year I was given the go-ahead to put together the University of Hartford radio station. I was appointed the general manager of it and I was given a full scholarship from the University of Hartford to go for it. There's a great engineering school at UH so the engineering statistics were put together by the director of the engineering school and his students. I was able to do all the programming. I was still doing weekends in Bristol, so I was considered a "professional." I was able to generate a lot of support. In high school I managed teams and was instrumental in getting "school spirit" projects off the ground. Doing the radio station was part of the same process. We got it on the air on July 15th, 1968. It took nine months to get the application through the FCC. We signed the station on with 1800 watts of effective radiation power. The call letters were WWUH.

Although we couldn't accept paid commercials, we got a few donations and we pulled some fast deals. You are allowed to acknowledge donations. We went to some car dealers and every time we did a newscast we said the news was compiled through the wire services of United Press International and the "mobile team in the Lippman Motors UH news wagon." Because we acknowledged Lippman Motors we got a news car, painted up with our call letters and WWUH license plates.

Before the station got started, a very generous man named Lewis Roth promised the then-president of the U of H that he would finance the radio station. Mr. Roth passed away before we got things rolling, but after we got the station off the ground his family came to us with a check for $50,000. We renamed the radio station the Lewis K. Roth Memorial radio station. When I left the radio station in 1970 we had a completely built stereo radio station, and still had $14,000 of Mr. Roth's grant left over.

Q. *Would you describe the early format of WWUH?*

A. To begin with, we went on the air from 6:00 p.m. to 1:30 a.m. We had an "easy listening" program for 45 minutes, 15 minutes of news and a feature called "Hartford Tonight" in which we recapped things that were happening around town. We programmed information from 7:00 to 7:30, jazz from 7:30 until 10, and progressive rock from 10:00 p.m. through sign-off. We ran opera on Sunday when we started weekend broadcasting.

For the first three weeks I had to run the board for ever show in order to train people.

Within a year we were broadcasting 24 hours a day, seven days a week. The response from the community was great.

Q. *One of the best times I ever had in radio was when your station let me play jazz on Wednesday nights for a couple of hours. Because I was then employed at WPOP I used a different name on the air each week. One week I was "Bill Drake," another I was "John Rook," and another I was "Paul Drew." It was an inside joke using the names of top radio programmers of that day. My "career" came to an end one day when my PD at the time, Dan Clayton (Ken Wolt) got a new car with an FM and recognized my voice on your station. You used a lot of outside people at your station. Why did you use them rather than U of H students?*

A. When you went on the air doing the jazz show it was wonderful. It sounded terrific, and using the inside joke names of the top radio programmers was a lot of fun. However, we did use outside people at our stations. One of the reasons the University was so pleased with us was the board of advisors group that we put together. You'll remember because you were one of our advisors. We showed them 12 or 14 area professionals who were going to be in contact with us. We could ask them questions. It made the University feel good, and although we never really had to go to the board for major decisions, we did have the feedback and we had interested people like yourself, and the late Morgan [*formerly of WCCC Radio Hartford, Morgan was killed a few years later in a plane crash with Jim Croce*] who would come in and spend some time with the students. We really designed the station for the students but it was nice to have area professionals come in and help build the quality of the sound of the radio station. That's why we used those people. We never neglected the students; they always had first shot, but because we were on the air 24 hours a day, seven days a week, there were times when people just said "I can't make it, I've got classes." We would use the outside people during exam periods and the like.

Q. *You went on to make a career in radio. Did some of the other people who pioneered that station also go on into broadcast as a career?*

A. Yes, some of the others did go on to radio. Randy Maier, who was with me at the beginning, became the first general manager of WHCN in Hartford. He took Neil Portnoy with him and two of them ran WHCN off the mountain (at the transmitter site) doing six hour shifts with two tape recorders, a turntable, and some equipment that disappeared from WWUH. Larry Titus, who was our original Chief Engineer, is still an engineer in the area. Ronnie Burger became the PD of WPLR in New Haven when it went on. Burger left radio to go into the record business for several years and now is selling insurance in the Philadelphia area.

Q. *During the years you were building and operating your college station, there was a great deal of activity at the college level. We heard lots of predictions that college radio would be the training ground for the new wave of air personalities. Record companies responded to the growth of college radio by creating promotion staffs designed to promote their product at the college level. There were a number of seminars held to encourage the growth of college radio. It's all gone. You hear very little about college radio today. With some notable exceptions, like WBRU in Providence, college radio has little or no effect on audience. Record companies have abandoned their promotion efforts to that market aside from maintaining mailing lists. I know of very few major radio personalities who came from that era. What happened? What happened to the dream you created and nurtured? Why has college radio failed to materialize as a force?*

A. There was a lot of talk back then about how college radio would develop the professional because this was a time when there were no media departments. It was not in vogue at the time to get into broadcasting or to take media courses. The closest thing we had at the U of H was a speech and drama department. Now just about every good school has a mass communications department. College radio, however, has changed. It really needs to have constant professional awareness.

I would go out and work weekends and get yelled at by a less-than-competent program director in some small market like Bristol, Connecticut, yet I knew what was right and what was wrong and I tried to teach my people that there was more to radio than just going on and trying to be Cousin Brucie [*Bruce Morrow, WABC-New York*].

As the music changed, people began to go on and play their own music. Discipline and direction at college stations is lacking. I think WWUH still is very valid in that community and does put a lot of people into professional radio and television. WBRU in Providence does a great job, too. A lot of college radio stations get lost in the shuffle because their programming is too varied and because their discipline is minimal. WERS is a fair example of that. They do a lot of jazz here. It's Emerson College, 20,000 watt stereo in Boston. They're all over the place. They also have WGBH and WBUR which are two big non-commercial stations in the market. It's just not as consistent or tight as it should be.

I think the dream that I was involved in is still there. What might have failed were individuals or individual general managers. I had an advantage because I was already a working professional and by the time I left WWUH I had been a TV director at two stations. I had worked at WPOP, WCCC, WRYM, WBIS, WCDQ, WDEE, WINF, a bunch of stations in the area. I'd been involved in a professional environment so I was a bit more demanding than the normal college general manager, who might have gotten the job because of a popularity contest, or maybe has never worked at a professional station. I think that is what is lacking at a lot of college stations. There are not a lot of professionals involved. The faculty advisor might have done radio several decades ago but they don't have the ongoing interest and direction to offer the students. The students themselves have not participated in real radio. I think those stations that are real broadcast stations, like WBRU and WWUH, do spawn the type of people who will go on into professional radio. WWUH was indeed a dream and it was unique from the beginning. That station, after 12½ years, still hasn't failed so I remain very proud of it. The program guide that's issued monthly looks good. I go through the area and punch it up and it sounds great. They've even kicked their power to 3000 watts off of Avon Mountain; WTIC gave them a place on their antenna farm.

Q. *When you're looking for somebody for your station does a college background mean anything to you?*

A. Today, as director of programming and promotion at WEEI-FM (a CBS-owned station in Boston), college radio means a great deal to me. I came to Boston ten years ago and started here at WBUR as assistant general manager and program director. I changed the station to stereo back then. I was in graduate school at the same time. I've employed interns at all of the stations I've worked. The intern help has been very beneficial and some of my interns have gone on to become big-time radio stars. I have a young lady with us now who started here a year ago and is now good enough to do all of the fill-in and weekends on WEEI-FM.

College radio does mean a lot to me but it means more if a student has done more than just gone in and played rock and roll records at three in the morning. A professional attitude has to come out of wherever you start your broadcast career. The actual hands-on experience of college is very important. If the direction is not there from the kid who's the manager, the drive, the professionalism, the determination, and the self discipline has to be within the individual. That can start in college radio.

Q. *After college you created a career for yourself in commercial broadcasting, especially in the Boston area. Tell us where you worked and in what capacities.*

A. I left Hartford in September of 1970 after working at six area stations, building WWUH-FM, and working as an on-camera reporter and director at Channels 8 and 30 in TV.

In Boston, my first station was WBUR at Boston University. After I withdrew from the B.U. graduate school program I remained at WBUR until June of 1971. In July of 1971 I was hired as the operations director of WBZ-AM and FM. It was like being the assistant PD to WBZ-AM. The FM was a throwaway but about four or five months down the line, Westinghouse decided they were going to do something with WBZ-FM. I was in charge of putting together the license renewal and changing the format from Middle of the Road (actually a mono fine arts station) to a Top 40 Teen Stereo Rocker. I organized the license renewal, set up the automation, the style, and the promotion. We went on with "All Hits, All the Time." I was the station coordinator. I was actually a one-person radio station until I got my friend Captain Ken Shelton to come to work for me as a management trainee for Westinghouse. The two of us continued to be WBZ-FM until I departed in June of 1975 because Westinghouse just wouldn't go commercial with it. I had done a lot with WBZ-FM over the 3½ years, but it was frustrating. With no commercials and a budget of $69,000 a year (which paid for my salary, Ken's salary, and the engineer's salary) we still brought it up to the seventh largest share and sixth largest cume in the market. We were second in teens. We had a 3.0 in ARB. We were ahead of WBZ-AM, WEEI-FM, WCOZ, WVBF, WROR, and WMEX. We did quite a number but Westinghouse just wouldn't support it.

In August 1975 I was hired by Dave Kroninger for WHDH, WCOZ. I was to be program manager and promotion director of WCOZ, which was a beautiful music station, owned by the John Blair company and by WHDH. It was "All Beautiful Music. All the Time, Stereo 94.5." I changed it to "Boston's Best Rock WCOZ 94½ FM." I went on the air and did afternoon drive from 4 to 7 and built the staff one by one. I ended up hiring five former program directors and four great women, three of whom were on the air. Then a new manager was put in. I had been reporting directly to Kroninger, who was the president/general manager of both WHDH and WCOZ. A business person was installed as station manager of WCOZ and he blew me out. It was a touch break. It was either a personality conflict or politics or he didn't want anybody around who knew more about the operation than he did. He was a young manager—33—and I was 26 and he wanted it to be "his." The station did very well without me. I left them with a very strong staff. For the year I was there I did programming, promotion, and afternoon drive.

Following WCOZ I was unemployed for six months. Nothing was happening. That's the way it often goes in this business.

I was brought back "from the dead" six months to the day after I had been fired to WEZE, an AM, 5000-watt station. It was floundering with a TM Middle of the Road music package. That's where I started "soft" rock. Although we never had ratings, I was so cranked up with ideas that we made a lot of noise and CBS came after me and gave me the job I had wanted ever since I came to Boston—Director of Programming and promotion for WEEI-FM. The station was then the "mellow sound." I came in, I called it soft rock, I put my rainbows all over town and in 3½ years I've been here we've done quite nicely. We're number one 25-34; we've been as high as a 5.1 share. Right now I'm at a 3.7. I just went live. We used to be on a computer. I used to program every cut 24 hours a day. We used to be "jock assist" over the automation. Now we're entirely live and I love it.

I'm also in charge of the promotion and many of the things I learned from you, Bob, I'm still doing.

Our station has quite a presence. I have soft rock directory cards, I have day-glow billboards all over town, I'm running TV spots using the rainbow. CBS is quite happy with us. We have the highest share of all of the CBS-FM stations.

Q. *You've done considerable work in the field of automated formats. Can you detail what, in your mind, are some of the advantages of automated formats?*

A. The two automated formats I worked with were at WEEI-FM and at WBZ-FM. We used the IGM "Instacart" system. This one at WEEI is more sophisticated than the one we had at WBZ-FM.

The advantage is that you can program it and if you cut the tapes speaking casually, it sounds like you are live. It's a long way from the "canned" sound that other automated stations have used. I do like live jocks. People make a big difference. The music is still very important. Preprogrammed music has something to be said for it, but I do want a live announcer.

Q. *What can you tell us about the format and the audience targets of WEEI?*

A. The format here is soft rock. It's a contemporary albums station but it's the "rock without the shock." We play Steeley Dan and Fleetwood Mac but we don't play the raucous things. We're playing everything from Streisand to Springsteen and blending it. Dayparting the station is important with one record flowing into another. There are a lot of oldies, some current singles, and a lot of cuts from album material. It's a nice sound that does target 25-34, where we are number one. Our overall consideration is 18-44. We have virtually no teenagers listening to this station. Last winter we had our highest book (5.1). We were number one in men 18-49, we were number one in adults 18-34, we were doing very well. We hit a slip; I lost two out of my four air people, they left me for more money. One went to WRKO and the other to WBCN.

Q. *Who are your main competitors in Boston?*

A. When you're talking 25-44 I've got to say that WHDH and WBZ are competitors. On the FM dial, WROR is a big factor because they've spent money. They've got five people in the morning and in the afternoon—a team doing news, weather, sports, traffic, and jock.

There is a lot of presence on WROR but they sound kind of dumb and the music is a little weird. A little station called WBOS tried disco and now is trying to do what I do but it's wimpy and doesn't have its act together. I think they will go country soon.

I consider anybody who has my audience in Boston as a competitor—anybody who has a piece of my prime demographic. There's a crossover with people who listen to WBCN, but not so much WCOZ anymore because they've gotten very hard.

Q. *On the surface it looks as though your career to date has been a breeze. You came out of college radio, went immediately into a big market situation, and remained there, successfully, for some time. What were the contributing factors to your seemingly instantaneous success?*

A. No, I don't think my career has been a breeze. I did go immediately into a big market situation, from Hartford to Boston, because I went to graduate school at WBUR, but I've worked full time on this for over 14 years now. Perseverance—being there, being interested, and being willing to work part-time shifts at weird hours, to do all-nights at WPOP when they'd call me or week-ends at WBIS, getting up at three or four o'clock in the morning every Saturday to go into that first job at WBIS—was hard work. I loved radio, I loved being on it, and I always liked managing. I managed sports teams in high school and was the public address announcer in high school and all the way back through grade school.

It's been a combination of hard work and having a pretty good idea of what I wanted to do. Growing up in New York City I was always very selective about what went on the radio. Being selective—looking for the top tracks and the best cuts—has made a difference. I never was a music junkie. I never said "We've got to play all of the Grateful Dead Album." When a new album like *Nashville Skyline* or *Crosby, Stills, and Nash* came out, you said "Wow, here's a cut called 'Guinevere,' and it's not a single; why don't we play it." When *Abbey Road* by the Beatles came out, nobody was playing "Here Comes the Sun" because it wasn't a single. It sounded like a single. You could do a talk over the intro. It was a hit. It was the Beatles. Why couldn't a radio station that played that kind of music happen? That was a thought I'd had since college and since the days of Peter, Paul and Mary and the Mamas and Papas. The Association and Fifth Dimension gave way to what "soft rock" is today. My career has been a matter of having an idea, and going for it.

Q. *I've always advised young students of broadcast that the road for them might be long and rocky. That road might include years in small towns and small markets working up to the bigtime. What do you tell these same students?*

A. I tell students that they do have to spend a lot of time looking around, paying their dues, working weird hours and the like. Being a DJ is rough because you don't get that big salary for quite a while. I didn't start to do well until I went to WBZ, not as the AM Operations Director (that job paid $11,500 in 1961), but when I went to FM where I had an increase plus an AFTRA position. Then I was making up around $20,000.

I often advise kids to think about sales if they really love broadcasting and if they don't have a great voice or special presence on the air. It takes a lot of work and the possibilities still do exist. There are possibilities today in television. There are more and more television stations and there are more opportunities for women.

I tell students that they have to pay their dues and, as it says in the song, "it don't come easy." They *can* do it, if they keep working.

Q. *To many students of broadcast, radio means music. They often consider that having a broad background in rock, for instance, will be a major asset in getting a job in radio. Can you respond to that? What kind of preparation for a broadcast career should the student seek to obtain?*

A. Rock and roll music is rock and roll music. Today rock and roll music means the B-52s, Kiss, and the Pretenders. When I grew up knowing rock and roll music, it was a time of "Maybe Baby" by Buddy Holly. It was the Beatles' *Rubber Soul*. Music has expanded. There are more and more radio stations. The glamour of being a Jonathan Schwartz or a Scott Muni is today what being Cousin Brucie was back then.

Not every radio station in the world is a progressive rock station. If you want to be a broadcaster you've got to be versatile. You can't expect to walk into the first station you work at and play what you want to play. There are still many stations playing Top 40, Pop-Adult, and Middle of the Road. If you don't know how to read a newscast and sound intelligent or be able to introduce Barry Manilow without barfing, you're in trouble. You've got to be able to be mainstream and versatile in what you do on the air. Being able to read a three-minute newscast is far more important than being able to name the tracks and engineers of the last Led Zeppelin album.

Experience is the best preparation—experience in all phases of the operation. Reading news, public affairs programs, writing public service announcements, and watching how a promotion with the sales department works. Radio is much more than music.

Q. *Are the colleges giving broadcasting students the kind of background and preparation they need to face the challenge of competitive commercial radio?*

A. I don't think colleges are giving broadcasting students what they need to go out and face commercial radio. I was excited about going to graduate school. They told me I was not suited for the Master's degree in broadcasting after one semester and suggested I withdraw. I was crushed at the time. They forbade me from taking courses in TV production because I'd been a professional TV director.

The big issue at that time was cable. Ten years later cable is not still the big issue. The big issue is good programming, good promotion, reaching the people, really serving the public's interest, convenience and necessity. I don't think there is enough emphasis on what real broadcasting is all about. Doing shows that win awards, doing shows that get ratings, doing shows that reach the people—that's what has to be instructed. They need practice in doing these programs and not the textbook junk. I really can't say enough about practical application—going out and trying it; making kids write up program schedules, having them do ascertainments, having them put together formats, and do market surveys.

Pose the question: "If you had a radio station, or control of any radio station in this market, what station would you take and what would you do with it?" Make them work with practical, real situations. I think that's what has to be done. That's what they are not doing. They're not paying attention to the practical, ongoing, professional things because the instructors, like the people who run college radio stations, simply don't have recent experience.

For a good broadcast school to have a good broadcast curriculum they should have outside professionals come in and help the students. I don't mean the schlock news director from the local Top 40 station. They should go after managers. They should go after group owners. They should go after people who really can give advice to the students. Emphasis has to be placed on making the student aware of a real environment. They have to be taught that radio is a business, a serious business, a money-making business and it's not just playing rock and roll records.

Q. College professors of communication seem to have had a lot of academic training and you've pointed out that most have had little actual radio programming experience. Talk a little more to that point.

A. That's the bottom line. They've all had academic experience, they've got PHDs, maybe they did a show on the Kansas State University station for a while, but they've never really done commercial broadcasting. Without commercial broadcast experience, these instructors won't be able to give proper guidance, the realistic guidance, the up-to-date guidance that is necessary for somebody to go in and deal with a program director, or general manager, or news director, or promotion manager to get a job in broadcasting today.

I think the best thing a student can do is to get involved in an intern program at a station. I started the intern program at Westinghouse, WBZ, in 1972. A student participates for 12 to 15 hours a week, sometimes full-time for a whole semester. We were involved with the University of Massachusetts, Harvard, Boston University, Boston College, Emerson, and a number of other schools on this project. The student gets course credit for participation. That, I think, is the best way to find out what a broadcast operation is all about. Participate at the station, get jobs to do at the station, get course credit while you're there and see what it's really like. That's the best step.

Other than that, the college needs to have a radio station that needs to act competitive. The station could be more valuable if it had a full-time professor, general manager of the station who had commercial broadcast experience. Such things are possible but I don't see it happening.

Right now it's up to the student to be as aware as possible and to realize that broadcasting is indeed a study and begin to go out and learn.

Q. What's your assessment of today's radio? Do you think it's relevant to the times? Is it serving the public interest? Is it doing something more than an "entertainment" function?

A. I think it's changing a lot; it's looking for a smaller piece of the pie and it's going right after it. It is serving the public interest? Sometimes. I think there is a lot more that radio can do. News radio stations indeed serve the public interest but I think it's also up to the music stations to have short features, little magazine drop-ins throughout their regular broadcast schedule that do address themselves to facts, to self-help, to services that are available. There are things that people should know about and radio can reach people on a one-to-one basis. It's not being done enough. There's too much emphasis on rock and roll and music and hype. There's not as much substance as there should be.

Q. Given the greatly expanded capacity of television in providing services and instantaneous news coverage, the role of radio as a news medium seems to be shrinking. Radio used to provide it "now" and newspapers used to provide the detail. I'd venture to say that most of the American public gets its main source of news each day from television. What's radio's function and future in news?

A. Television certainly has expanded. In spite of the fact that most of the American public gets most of its news from television I think radio is still immediate because radio is so portable. People have radios in places where they don't have televisions. Because of this, radio can be personable and personal. It can be one-to-one. It can be with you in a car, a boat, in the office, all the places where television is not commonly found. I think headline news and magazine features and a recap of some of the things that are not hard news is where radio has a part to play. If we spend two minutes to talk about the disposal of hazardous waste, I think we're providing a public service. That's an issue of concern, it's important to our target demographic, it's accepted by our demographic. However, I don't think you're going to hear a feature on disposal of hazardous waste in newscasts or on a regular basis on television. This is one of those "alternative magazine" type directions that I think radio can go in.

A two-minute piece on how to cure the common cold, going into the winter season, even if you tell people to have a gimlet and some chicken soup, causes people to think, to get a little bit of extra personal information. Radio can still be that warm, one-to-one, sincere friend. That's what continues to make radio special.

Combine the magazine type of approach and instant headlines. When news happens you still hear it on the radio first because TV is very scheduled, selective, and very stationary. Radio is everywhere, all the time.

Q. If you had an AM facility in Boston today, what would you do with it? FM provides Boston with music, low commercial content and fidelity. Several big wattage AMs continue to provide information and talk features. Assuming you were one of the FCCs newly created AM facilities, what's left to offer Boston?

A. I might refer you to John E. Garabedian who used to be on WMEX as the program director in the early '70s. He's got a construction permit and is about to kick on 25,000 watts at 1060 on the dial. WBZ is 1030. He signed on his facility with 1000 watts daytime. He's built quite an antenna farm and he's going to do something very interesting. Cousin Brucie is calling it FOR—Family Oriented Radio—around the New York City area.

I think AM still has a good shot. WHDH is doing a very nice job with the way they pick their music. They play a lot of jukebox oldies, and information and news. I think that's pretty good.

I might do telephone talk that's all self-help. Constant help radio working out people's problems, giving folks a chance to talk. It would be an old person's radio station that would be wonderful for people 50-plus—a format helping older folks who have nowhere else to go.

Telephone talk was a big thing for a while until the sex talk shows gave it all a bad name. It sort of floated away after that but I think there are still niches for AM radio stations. I'm sold on FM; it's fidelity and it's signal reach. I think you can do all the great things that AM radio *used* to do on FM. I'm trying to create a combination of a beautiful music WJIB of the '80s while at the same time being a hip one-to-one modernization of all the services that WBZ-AM used to do. We're doing it with movie reviews, we're doing it with magazine features, we're doing it with event happenings, reports of what's going on around the city.

If AM has its act together, plays the right music, has the right lifestyle, and knows who their target audience is, I think they can still come up with a niche and do a decent job.

Q. *As a last question, do you have a piece of advice for young broadcasters, or broadcast students, about to enter the business of radio?*

A. I would like to impress upon young broadcasters and students that broadcasting is a *business*. It's extremely self-serving and enjoyable and romantic to be on the air, and project your voice and play your favorite records, but radio is a business and you've trying to reach as many people as you can at all times. Without the audience, you don't have any value to the broadcast.

The more people that listen, the more money you can charge for the commercial time that's offered and that's how it works.

Broadcasting on the performing side takes a lot of work. Read out loud at home, constantly, practice sight reading, practice different styles of delivery, get to the point where you're as conversational, real, and understandable on the radio as you would be sitting around talking to somebody one to one. It's basic human communication.

It takes a lot of work. It takes a lot of strange hours. It takes a lot of practice to get the style to be a marketable commodity to a professional broadcast station. Small markets and college radio are great places to start. Get as much practice as you can before trying to invade a big station.

When you're interested in applying to a station, listen to it for a couple of days. Nothing makes you look more dumb than addressing a letter to a station in your area as "Attention: Program Director." You live in the area; pick up the phone and call to find out the person's name. Find out, what the station is like. Don't send a Top 40 aircheck to an MOR radio station. Don't send a progressive rock tape to a station that only plays Carole King and Joni Mitchell. Try to understand what the station is about. Be versatile but don't say "I'll do anything." Say "This is what I can do and I think you need this." Then, if they say they need something else, you say "I can do that, too." Or, "I'd be happy to adjust my talents to that direction because I'd like to work at your radio station."

People send out tapes that are tails out and wrapped so tightly it's like a Chinese jigsaw puzzle to get the tape onto the machine. Make it as easy as possible for the PD to listen to your tape.

Don't send tapes out blindly saying "hire me." Don't take anything for granted. Sometimes students say "I've done three semesters of radio; give me a job." It takes time, it takes work, it takes patience, and it takes an understanding of what's going on. If you're just starting out perhaps you should try to get a job as an intern.

This is a business of fast-talking hypersters but like everything else, if you have the facts and you have the confidence you'll do well.

Tom Shovan

Tom Shovan is an outrage. He is too big, too boisterous, too talented—in fact, Tom Shovan is too much of everything.

He weighs in excess of 400 pounds and I know him well enough to know that all that bulk, which would be an embarrassment and an encumberance to sombody else, exists in Tom Shovan because it takes that much space to hold the sheer warmth of the man.

"Show Biz" often makes the successful hard, cynical, cruel, and thoughtless. Rumor has it that it's one of the prices we pay to get ahead in a competitive business filled with insecure people. If that's the price, I don't think Tom Shovan could pay it—or would pay it if he could. For those of us who know him, we'd just as soon have it that way.

You'll learn a lot from the following pages—about radio and about people.

Q. For those readers who may not be familiar with your background, would you please tell us about some of the towns you've worked and the stations you've worked for?

A. I started in my hometown station, WKXL in Concord, New Hampshire, and worked the New England radio circuit early in my career. Radio in small towns always paid poorly and I loved being on the air so the combination had me working on multiple stations at the same time—usually without any station knowing of the other having me on the payroll. Nobody used his own name in those days on the air. My record was five stations at once: mornings in Sanford, Maine, middays-early afternoon in Portland, Maine, evenings in Portsmouth, Saturday and Sunday evenings in Portland doing booth announcing, and an all-night show Sunday nights in Portland, Maine.

As far as stations of note are concerned, I worked at some of the "hit" Northeast rockers in their heyday, including WMEX in Boston when it was Boston's number one station and WHIL in Medford (a Boston suburb) when they had the "Tiger Radio" rock format in the late '50s with substantial Boston ratings. An interesting sidelight is that this station copied the early McLendon radio right down to the "Musical Newscasts" with the dramatic stagings and sound effects.

I also worked for a time at WCOP in Boston when they were rocking. I was at WPOP in Hartford, WINS in New York City just before they switched to all-news, WPTR in Albany, WJAB in Portland, Maine, one of the early rock successes, a daytimer with four full-time competitors in town on AM and licensed to Westbrook, Maine, which pulled ratings of over 50% of the audience!

Other stations include CJAD-Montreal, Quebec, WKBR-Manchester, WFEA-Manchester, WORL-Boston, WICE-Providence, WABB-Mobile, Alabama, and so forth ad nauseum.

Q. *One of your trademarks was your size. As I remember, you were once billed as the "World's Largest Disk Jockey." I've even heard an outrageous story about you being floated down the river on a barge. Tell us that story.*

A. Weight—at one time mine topped 450 pounds—can either be an inhibiting factor or an asset. Programming genius Dick Lawrence, who built WKBE into a rock success, made little 250 WABY number one in the Albany market about 1960 when the station couldn't even be heard in half the survey area and ran up a roster of other big success stories, sat me down and helped me come to the conclusion to use my size as an advantage—and it really worked for me. I became "The World's Largest Disk Jockey" and never lost my title. I was challenged a couple of times—even hired one of the challengers to jock at a station I was consulting at the time. As the "World's Largest DJ." I used to use giant-sized props on personal appearances—lighting enormous cigars with a mammoth cigarette lighter, huge comb, toothbrush and assorted props. Cloth manufacturer H-I-S Company custom-made their products for me as promotion gratis—which was great for me as stylish big clothes are hard to find.

When I later went to work for Dick Lawrence at WPTR, we really let loose with the "World's Largest" stuff. Promos on the air with sound effects that the studio was being rebuilt and reinforced for me, all culminating with floating me into town on a barge on the Hudson River barge canal, lifting me off with a derrick and hauling me on a flatbed to the station. Nobody does this kind of thing any more!

Q. *As I remember, when you worked in Boston, you worked for one of the Top 40 radio pioneers. One of the elements of his station was the Top 40 radio pioneers. One of the elements of his station was the "house" name. Tell us about Max Richmond and about your "house" name.*

A. Love him or hate him, most radio people have an opinion about Max Richmond. Max and his brother owned WMEX in Boston and Max ran it with an iron fist. Max was one of the Top 40 pioneers. Lifting a little Todd Storz, a little McLendon, a little Duncan Mounsey and a little of anyone else who was developing Top 40 ideas, and adding his own ideas, Max had a red-hot station. WMEX—whose call letters indicated the heavily Spanish format—was running racing results, treasury balance figures and about every other daily number and bettable figure on the air. They had a large bank of phones, allegedly operating one of Boston's biggest bookmaking services at the time of their raid and sudden format change in the '50s. Max's initial format was a fast rotation of the hottest hits and a reasonably large list of new songs exposed inbetween. Virtually everything the jock said was on the blackboard, 3 × 5 cards, or dictated by Max. The pay was dirt and the turnover was unbelievable—partly to keep everyone from staying long enough to be eligible for unionizing, partly animosity for Max, partly because of working conditions.

The station was then on the second floor walkup next to Fenway Park. One would walk up a flight of filthy, dingy stairs, down a hall covered with graffiti, lipstick kiss marks from adolescent female fans and other assorted smears from innumerable sources. As you entered the station lobby you could see the studios through dirty windows while a receptionist tried to keep the viewing audience's stay as brief as possible as she popped her bubble gum. Max, meanwhile, would stroll into the lobby from time to time and quiz the fans about what they liked and didn't like about the station and its people. On more than one occasion, some major decisions were made based upon these "surveys."

Because of the turnover and Max's opinion that nobody gives a damn about the jock anyhow, just the name, Max created a roster of station names. His first morning man, Joe Thomas, used his real name and when he left after hordes of promotion, Max said "Never again." From then on, for years, the morning man was always named "Fenway"—no first name no last, just Fenway, of course after Fenway park, the Boston Red Sox ballfield. The midday man was always "Dan Donovan" and I think the last Dan Donovan was the 28th or 29th to bear that name. Lots of them retained that name when they left and still use it. Mel Miller was one of WMEX's originals and used his own name. When he left early in WMEX's rock history for Canada, Max phased him out and named his successor Mel, alternating between records with Melvin. This evolved into Melvin X. Melvin as a house name for a couple of weeks. Later on, Mel Miller came back using his own name on the air while the house name Melvin X. Melvin continued as well. There were fewer Melvin X. Melvins of which I was one.

The nights belong to Arnie "Woo Woo" Ginsburg—the "Woo-Woo" coming from his assortment of bells, whistles, and horns he used throughout the show. Really late night (after Arnie's show ended at 10:00—that's late in New England) was talk, done for years by Jerry Williams.

Max Richmond himself was a character. I happen to have liked him and I think he liked me, but one could never tell. He was gruff, uncouth, dressed in baggy, unstylish clothing, cheap, opinionated and dictatorial . . . but he knew radio! He loved cliches and rhymes and slogans. When he'd come up with a new one he'd buzz the studio or come in and get it on the air fast and often. He'd call at the first drop of rain screaming "Dammit, start saying When It Rains, We Shine!" Max loved jingles; he bought just about every package from everybody. The salesmen liked him but the jingle operators hated him because of his extensive relyricing. He localized every jingle, had singers sing over the opening, closing pauses—the poetic phrasing was long, often clever sometimes brilliant—but it wasn't what the jingles were written to sound like. WMEX jingles are unique to say the least. Jody Lyons (the father of PAMS jingles who wrote, created, arranged, etc., most of the great jingles of history and is now writing hit songs and scores) told me just this week he'd never forget what Max Richmond at WMEX used to do to his jingles. It still makes him cringe.

Q. *When you worked in a small market, Hyde Park, New York, it was after working in some pretty good stations. You were able to bring into that small town the benefit of your previous experience and a radio station like they'd never heard before. As I remember, you didn't have much of a promotion budget but you promoted constantly. For some of our readers who find themselves in the same situation, tell us about some of the novel promotions you introduced in that market, the kinds of prizes you offered, and a little about what your promotion budget amounted to.*

A. There's a lot of turnover in jocking—not just because the jock wants to leave or the PD is tired of the jock or even the book is bad. Whenever there's a rumble at the top—new owner, GM, PD, or even sales manager—there are jock changes. I decided I wanted to get into administration and was romanced into taking the position of vice-president of operations of the Star Group. They owned WEEE in Albany, WKIP and WSPK-FM in Poughkeepsie, WBJA-TV in Binghamton, and a purchase option on WRNY in Rome, N.Y. Corporate headquarters were in Poughkeepsie, and it was a management job with what looked like a lot of security and stability. However, the corporation president fled the coop with the money of a lot of "heavies" who'd invested in the undertaking, including actor Eddie Bracken and textile magnate Oliver Lazare. In the dust I temporarily went to the aid of a long-time friend who I'd met earlier in the New England radio circuit who owned a little station in Hyde Park (just outside of Poughkeepsie, which he'd built from scrap parts he'd received in lieu of cash payment for doing engineering consulting for stations around the Northeast. He'd found the frequency himself and as an engineer built it. I told him I'd put the programming in order . . . temporarily. I ended up like the guy who came to dinner, except I raised, prepared, and cooked the dinner too—and washed the dishes. I programmed the station (WHVW) and helped him build an FM to go with it. He was a full-time college professor so I ended up taking over management. We built the station into quite a phenomenon. We were responsible for "breaking" a number of hit records—a real bellweather station for exposing new product and looked to by most of the major trade publications—unusual for a small station. We developed a lot of new talent; we took a local milkman and taught him radio and he's now a WABC mainstay. We fed jocks to other radio stations like CKLW, WOR-FM, WPRO, WCFL, and lots of other majors.

Smaller stations generally don't have promotion budgets as such. In fact, the use of cash for promotion is a real problem. As a GM I would sometimes write a promotion budget into a sales promotion so we could pay for a tie-in, but most of the promotion we did was trade-out. We did a lot of promotion; we had billboards we traded out either directly or through a second party who had a billboard commitment and didn't need them all or could be dissuaded from using them all. We did pay for the paper used on the billboards in cash. We traded out cars, cruises, etc., for giveaways too.

But to explain the mainstay of my Hyde Park promotions I must point out a couple of things. First, promotion must reflect the market and its people. Hyde Park people are "plain folk." Lots of them are volunteer firemen; they hunt, play bingo at the town hall, and they don't want a lot of fancy fast talk. They want to have fun. You *must* know your market or you'll die.

Secondly, I always remember what Max Richmond once told me: a lot of stupid stations give away a diamond ring and make it sound like they just gave away—ho-hum—a 25¢ ballpoint pen. The secret is to give away junk and make the listener think you just gave away a million bucks through the excitement of the damn thing. Only one person wins the prize so only he knows how crappy it is and the rest of the listeners have to win in some other way . . . and they're the important ones because they're the mass audience so they've got to either win themselves or share the fun and the excitement so thoroughly that they're winners, of sorts.

Our audience had fun, win or lose, and with our prizes on our smaller-running promotions, whether you got the prize or not didn't matter all that much.

I guess our best known classic was during the toilet paper shortage of the early '70s. We traded out cases of toilet paper for "The Great Toilet Paper Rip-Off." I loved rotating cartridge contests—the roulette wheel principle. In this one, the random caller was put on the air as a sexy girl started tearing sheets off a roll of toilet paper for her unspecified use. The listener was to yell "stop" after any tear and thus won the number of rolls of precious, scarce paper that equalled the number of sheets hitherto torn off. However, if the toilet flushed before the listener yelled stop, then the winnings went down the toilet. This kind of contest would be a disaster in a sophisticated New York suburb like White Plains or Briarcliff Manor but it was a sensation in Hyde Park.

On Halloween, listeners drove 20 miles and more to pick up their prize. (We *never* mailed out prizes—that way we'd only actually circulate about 60% of the prizes awarded. The listeners really wanted to just win and have their names on the air.) The Halloween prize was a WHVW mini-monster—the kind of rubber gnomes that roll out of gumball-type machines in supermarkets for mommy's nickel. I don't tell this to say we were bilking our listeners—nobody complained—it was the packaging of the contest, the feeling that they had won something that had *magic*—not intrinsic value per se, but it was part of the radio station that in turn was part of their lives.

In rural Hyde Park, skunk carcasses line the roads like panhandlers in New York or star map salesmen in Hollywood, and when Loudan Wainwright's "Dead Skunk" was a hit record, Hyde Park identified with it . . . and WHVW had our listeners call and predict how many carcasses of dead skunks our Stinkmobile was going to roll over on the prerecorded cartridge tape. I don't remember the prize, but I know it wasn't worth much and the phone company complained we were blowing out circuits because of the phone responses every time we ran the promotion . . . and again, no complaints.

These are the zany ones, and we did a load of them. They made the station fun to listen to. The "taste" question had to be carefully determined market by market, but the idea that a station can have a promotion on little or no budget and a lot of fun is something sorely missing today.

Then too, there's the vital community involvement. President Franklin Roosevelt came from Hyde Park and I ran every January a "Mile of Dimes" from Roosevelt's home in Hyde Park. The circular driveway to the home was exactly one mile long into the house from the highway and back to the street. January is March of Dimes month and we had listeners drive through with their contributions to the March of Dimes all day as we broadcast live, moving along the driveway through the day, playing no music, just interviewing donors and presenting entertainment from the site. The first year we actually Scotch-taped the dimes, ten to the foot, into strips and laid them down the driveway. I learned the logistics of $5280 in dimes the hard way—and the unbelievable task of getting the damn dimes out of the tape afterward which had to be done by a chemical factory. In later years I had the strips printed with pictures of dimes which we laid down along the driveway as we went. Why January? It's cold in January but that's half of what made the listeners love us, and it was March of Dimes Month! Somebody up there liked us, because I always scheduled it for the next-to-last Sunday in January (that gave me a snow date still in January in case of a storm) and it never snowed in the eight years I did it and it never was bitterly cold that day. The year I left, the new owners of WHVW stopped the event and there was a blizzard and a half on the Sunday the promotion would have been scheduled.

Q. *It's obvious that a creative programmer can make up in creativity what he lacks in promotion dollars. What was the favorite promotion you've participated in, either as a jock or as a PD?*

A. It's hard to single out one promotion as a creative favorite but if I had to narrow it down to one it would probably be one we did in Albany. We used a new employee of WPTR as a "front man" to rent a storefront in Albany as a fortune-telling establishment. Furnishings were inexpensive yet sparkling and the sign was erected "Wonderful Juan." The nature of "Wonderful Juan's" exact business remained unclear but there was little doubt it was not just a fortune teller, phrenologist, or soothsayer. Wonderful Juan was not only brilliant but apparently also had a retail business of some kind yet to be disclosed, and an advertising budget beyond compare.

In fact, for weeks before "Wonderful Juan" even opened his door, spots were running on WPTR and WPTR's competitors saying "Wonderful Juan is coming and your life will never be the same . . . " etc. They were very cleverly worded spots that built great excitement and heralded a live remote to be broadcast simultaneously on every contemporary station in the market on "Wonderful Juan's" opening day. Press releases appeared, news stories, speculation, but no further information.

The day and the moment of "Wonderful Juan's" grand opening finally arrived and the mikes of the various stations were set up in Juan's sparkling front room amid mirrors, photographers, gold leaf logos, etc. The seconds ticked down to starting time and while assistants abounded in hospitality, Wonderful Juan was nowhere to be seen. Each station was instructed to open the remote with its own excitement and then on cue to all, announce "Now, the moment you've been waiting for—Wonderful Juan is here!" At that moment, right on cue, a turbaned figure in a robe came through the curtain and strode to microphones saying something to the effect that, "Yes Wonderful Juan is here . . . *Wonderful Juan Five Four Oh,* 1540 WPTR; we're at one-five-four-oh on your dial and what we're doing will change your listening habits, your whole life . . . tune us in . . . " etc. Flashbulbs flashed and the stations started chopping off the remote, but only well after the promotion had been aired. The upshot of the whole thing is that it was probably the most talked-about promotion I've ever seen. Since the stations cut off the remote *in violation of the contract,* WPTR never had to pay for the remotes or the pre-promotion. All it cost was a few days rent on a storefront and it was a spectacular lead to the new logo "Wonderful" 1-5-4-0."

Q. *In the course of your growth in radio you made the transition from air personality to program director to general manager. What was the hardest adjustment you had to make in moving from staff to management?*

A. I think the hardest adjustment I ever had to make from staff to management was to "let go" of areas and to delegate. When I first started programming I wanted to stay on the air, voice all the promos, oversee and pick all the music for everybody, listen constantly to the station and nitpick. I gave myself a "backup jock" or "second announcer on duty" shift sign-on to sign-off seven days a week. It took being in the hospital for a few days for a minor operation and being out of the day-to-day station activity to realize I was supposed to oversee, not live it all. Life became easier for me and, I'm sure, the staff. As a GM I had to hand over PD reins and though I knew enough to do it, it was still hard. Record people I'd known for decades came in and hyped me on records, wanted favors, lunched me and continued our personal relationship. How do you tell them you don't do anything with the music, ever, even for a friend? How do you ask the PD to listen again to a record—which I just don't believe in doing. I was castrated by management unneccessarily through the years because of the GM's ego, and from their side of the picture I'm sure they felt justified. I've tried to hire people I trust, then trust them to do what they were hired for. It's hard and always will be, partly because I've lived their mistakes and can foresee a lot of problems. To remove their right to "touch the wet paint" after the sign has been pointed out is to remove their self-respect.

Q. *In small markets like Hyde Park and Milford your station faces a lot of competition. Large market radio slices away at your audience and newspapers hack away at your client list. I expect you've had a lot of opportunity to practice some "creative" selling techniques. Since a lot of small and medium market*

PDs may find themselves in this situation tell us a little about it and how you handled it.

A. Creative selling techniques in highly competitive markets could fill five volumes and not scratch the surface. The Bridgeport/New Haven market, for example, has more radio stations on the AM/FM dial than any other place on the North American continent according to FCC figures. Selling a suburban daytimer there is a real challenge.

First, in any market, I try and make the radio station an integral part of the community—visible at all community functions, involving all community groups possible, getting all employees involved in civic functions, picking up on local problems and helping raise support, money, etc. We ran radiothons, MD carnivals, parades, charity home shows, scads of charity remotes. Whatever we did, we sold. I also packaged radio with other media, shared billboard space, placemats, road maps, bumper stickers, store-door stickers, and coupon books. If the prospective advertiser didn't like radio (or our station) I'd find out what he did like, no matter what it was and tie it in a package with the station. Then he'd buy the station as par of the package. The second time around he was an easier sell.

Q. *In Hyde Park and in Milford you also had to concern yourself with engineering. In fact, in Milford you relocated the station and redesigned the office, studio and engineering space. How did you get into engineering and, aside from dollars, what were some of the biggest problems you had?*

A. I've always prided myself with having a knowledge of all facets of the station operation. When I started in radio, before my hometown station hired me at age 12 on the air, I spent two previous years at the transmitter building. The FCC hadn't approved remote control operation of stations yet and engineers sat at the building in the swamp. For lack of anything to do, most of them either built ham gear or repaired radios on a contract basis for shops and hotel chains. I learned how to help repair radios and a little about engineering. Subsequently I studied toward a First Class license but never had the time to complete the study. The technology kept moving faster than my reading so I still have no license. I do have a reasonably practical working knowledge.

In Hyde Park I had a crackerjack engineer. He was a recruit pulled from the station's Explorer Scout troop and he learned on the job. He's still one of the sharpest engineering minds I know. That station was built from spare parts and I just kept updating as profits permitted.

Milford, Connecticut is a nightmare I'd sooner forget. My first day as GM I was shown an eviction notice from the studios dated four years earlier. No rent had been paid for years. Under terrific pressure of time I traded out a modular home, built a concrete single-story structure the same size as the modular home on the transmitter site, then set the home on top, built a stairway, panelled, carpeted, and connected the parts. I had a two-story building—operations downstairs, offices upstairs. Not big, but it was ours.

Our old studios were unbelievable. We were in a shopping center.

153

There was a huge "community" room rented by the hour to anyone who wanted it for meetings, dances, classes, band practice, etc. The station was in four closet-style rooms off this large room, one in each of the four corners—no windows, no ventilation, no signs, nothing! The station itself was, I'm told, improperly engineered. Construction and maintenance were unheard of. When I arrived, twelve years after it went on, it was barely on the air. Finding, hiring, retaining, and hand-holding engineers was a full-time job. We had no credit from any supplier and the owner considered engineering of lowest priority. Long before I came and probably for perpetuity the station was one of the FCC's engineering nightmares. Though I'm told we did more to get that place in shape in any given month than had been done in the preceding twelve years, it was a hard fight.

Q. *I can always remember your control rooms. They were littered with signs tacked all over the room instructing the jock about time checks, tag lines, current promotions, music formats and the information on your hot clock. You don't see much of that anymore. Why did you do it that way, and do you feel that the way they do it today has caused radio to lose some of its excitement?*

A. My format fit my staff and stations. In Albany, for example, I didn't line the walls with the horde of signs and memos at WEEE that I did in Hyde Park. Wall Street Journal writer Jonathan Kwitney did a feature on my format structuring in Hyde Park. One of the points he made is that a small station must recruit inexperienced talent and train them. In learning to read, write, speak a new language, or whatever, the person must be guided—must repeat over and over from a form or example; copy letters, pronounce words. It's the same with learning radio—build the skeleton. I built a station anyone could sound pretty good on just by following directions. Then, individually, I'd work with the jocks to allow them certain latitude within the structure. No station sounds good without direction. If you've got a staff of seasoned pros with decades of experience, jock meetings can often determine that course and little written material is needed. For me and my purposes, I was often best able to assure proper direction of the station through making that outline clear and indisputable. I think today many programmers only know they want quarter hours, numbers, and results but don't really know what direction they want their station to go, what they want people to think about it. They scream about hot clocks and liner cards and slogons but I know one L.A. station with a four-page memo on how to rotate jingles. PDs still direct but the priorities are different and the thinking is different.

Q. *In small markets the problem of finding talent is a big one. Salaries are such that you often can't attract talent away from other stations. Consequently, you have to find talent and train it. Tell us some of the problems involved in this aspect of smaller market radio.*

A. I always spent a lot of time on talent—finding newcomers, training them, then pushing them out of the nest on to bigger things. Thus, with a roster of heavy alumni call letters I was able to continue the cycle. I like to think I have a lot of friends in programming and a reasonable credibility, so when I'd call a Bob Paiva at WPOP, Johnny Canton at WDGY, or whatever and say I had a guy ready for him, he'd get the gig. There was a lot of turnover in that way but nowhere near as much as happens other ways. A guy would stay longer if he felt he was going somewhere and was being worked with, and the people I had sounded good.

Q. What is the most common technical, or attitudinal problem you found in recruiting new talent?

A. Looking at the smaller markets, there are generally three types of people in the available supply of air talent: relatively inexperienced people, experienced people who have remained in the small/medium market orbit and floated for a period of time, and finally the "over-the-hill gang"—drunks, outdated acts, ex-cons and other former major market talent that hit bad times and crashed and are now available for anything. Of the three available types I usually look to the inexperienced and develop them.

The biggest hitch is that there are no decent training grounds to pre-train broadcasters. The broadcast schools are anywhere from blatant ripoffs to equivalent of two weeks on a Burger King order microphone. Often a new jock needs to be deprogrammed from preconceived radio "knowlege" he may have obtained at some unstructured toilet that was his first job. They all expect stardom; they all have insecurities, and need to be helped. I've hired "chronic" drifters from the small market circuit and found that all they needed was understanding.

I hired a great newsman who had never worked longer than 90 days anywhere, but he was a good worker and a nice guy. Talking to his previous employers I got the same story. He seemed self-destructive and wanted to quit or get let go after he'd been at the station a while and he'd worked at dozens of stations. We interviewed and went to lunch. I laid out the facts as I knew them. We frankly discussed the problem, and we decided we'd work on the solution together and that he'd level with me when he felt the pressures. We made a chart of how long he'd stayed at each place he'd worked. When he'd been at my station for one of these "milestones" we had a celebration—a ribbon, a champagne toast, whatever. That 90-day record became a real target. When we reached 90 days we had a staff party, and gave him a "non-retirement" Mickey Mouse watch. He was still at the station 3½ years later when he accepted an excellent major market job. Talent needs somewhere to learn what a career in radio is really going to be like, and a real preparation for it. They also need station administration with the time and sensitivity to deal with their needs.

Q. As I remember, you were always able to keep a high level of energy within your staff. What was your key to keeping your air personalities motivated?

A. I believe a high level of energy is necessary in a station—*positive* energy, that is. One cannot push a rope. The rope must be pulled. I always spent a lot of time in the station, including weekends. I always worked a shift on Christmas and New Year's. I came in at unpredictable times, spent a lot of time with the jocks and newspeople when I was programming, went to lunch a lot with them, pulled up a chair in the studio on a slow day. I empathised and involved myself with the staff and their problems on the positive side.

On the other hand, I monitored constantly and when I was out of town I had the station randomly airchecked. I also had a self-telescoping aircheck machine going constantly, activated whenever the mike went on. I listened to tapes often and critically, and gave positive suggestions and gave them Hell when they fell apart.

There's never been any question what I wanted out of a performer. When I hire anyone, I tell them I'm opinionated and I want things done my way. I'll listen to suggestions, but unless we decide up front that something's to change, my way goes, *period*. I lay everything out up front. I had a bound operations manual and made new employees read it thoroughly before accepting the job. No surprises—everybody always knows where he stands at all times.

I think everybody knew we had a good sound—bigger than the market—and a good national reputation, that the audience loved the station, and they were developing their careers toward bigger and better markets and positions, so they were constantly up. They knew we cared from within and others outside were watching too. The staffers and I socialized a lot. It was fun and they believed in what they were doing.

Q. *You were part of the radio days when a promotion might mean sitting a disk jockey on a flagpole for 30 days and music meant trying to stay ahead of the other guy's introduction of a new group or a new song. It was certainly in the days before computers and a lot of the fancy research being done today. In retrospect, do you think that a station, operated in the way it used to be done, could survive in today's radio market?*

A. There is little question in my mind that radio today is unexciting. I don't see radio today as being part of the lives of the American people the way it used to be. Recently we did some interviews at a grade school with youngsters ages 5-10 for a show I was producing. In the course of the questioning the kids asked what the interviews were for and I replied they would be on the radio. None of the youngsters were particularly thrilled by this prospect except for a couple who showed a mild interest. One asked, "then that means I'll be able to hear myself in the car, huh?." Further questions determined that this group thought of radio as existing almost *solely in automobiles.* All I'm saying is that radio isn't listened to anymore. It's being *heard.* We've eliminated the negatives until there's nothing left. We've turned an art into a science. I don't think pulling a Max Richmond, Gordon McLendon, Tom Shovan, or any other format *per se* out of mothballs and putting it on the air would work today, but putting a little pizazz into radio could only help. Instead of quarter-hour current audience maintenance, perhaps more attention toward attracting new people through fun, excitement and diversity of program content might be the answer.

You ask a child what she wants and she'll say ice cream and chocolate cake, take away the vegetables. If you want to keep a child thrilled for the moment, give her what she *thinks* she wants. But in the long run you wind up losing. Radio's done that. Research has its place but radio is an art form and it deals with too many intangibles to ever be a science. I think we can profit from research. One thing we've learned today is to understand the market and the audience and then decide what you want to *sound like* and *be thought of as*, then *do it*. The devil with stats.

Q. *You've made another transition in your career. You've gone from general manager of a radio station to running the sales and marketing function of a record company. Why did you make the move? Wasn't radio bringing you satisfaction anymore or did you see the new challenge as more exciting?*

A. Primarily I left radio because of a tremendous opportunity to head sales and marketing for Wayne Newton at the inception of his brand-new record company. The money, the fringe benefits, and the experience itself added up to something one only can hope for a shot at once in a lifetime. To pass it up would be something I'd look back on and wonder about the rest of my life. The offer came at a good time in that I was frustrated with radio. I had turned around a twelve-year losing radio station to a healthy profit-maker and the owner was looking to unload it. Should I keep building the station so it could be sold at a profit and start again in a new market? That's like being a jock and getting good numbers then moving on when the PDs change.

Do you go to a corporate setup and start playing the statistics game and throw away the imagination and creativity and be one of those trying to turn an art into a science to justify his every action?

I love radio—the affair started before puberty—and often I'm afraid it's going to predecease me, and that's sad. I even think at times of going back and trying to do something to help, but I'm not sure what that would be.

Q. *Looking at radio from the other side and dealing with program directors from all over the country from the record side of the business, has your attitude, or opinion, of radio changed?*

A. Program directors are facing big problems today. Some know they are, some don't. Many PDs are inexperienced and many aren't really programming at all, they're just concerned with the jock lineup, playlist, scheduling of IDs and spots. Many PDs are sharp and yet restricted by their superiors, the FCC, and the fear of going out on a limb.

My biggest disillusionment when I entered the record industry was the music directors—the seriousness with which they often take themselves, the prima donnas, the lack of flexibility and the pomposity. I don't mean to indict a whole industry of music directors, but the industry has made so many of them crazed. It's so vital to a record promoter to get his record on a station that he patronizes and strokes the music directors beyond all reason, *anything* for a play. The music directors are usually young, and like most of the people who've chosen the performing arts as a career, somewhat insecure. Perhaps they lacked peer acceptance in youth. Now they're the central figure in the lives of a whole bunch of record people who are showering them with attention, tickets, gifts, and God knows what else

They're no more ready for that than was Freddy Prinze for TV. It's not their fault. A lot of them grow out of it or learn the hard way that when they lose their gig and look to their "friends" in the record business that they get the cold shoulder.

I think there is too much emphasis on the music director in the station and with imagination should also come diversification of music selection responsibilities. This is not a generalization. Some of the most gentlemanly, courteous, and astute radio people I have encountered are music directors, but I've also encountered a lot of people who have grossly misused the power that comes with that position.

Q. *I found when I was in the record business that I listened to radio in a different way. I listened to find out what they were playing and not so much for what they were doing. Did you find the same thing happening to you?*

A. When I entered the record business I shut off the radio altogether at first. Now I listen both to hear what's being played and as the eternal critic. I'm afraid I'll always counter-program in my mind, quarterback, and analyze. Sadly, though, there's very little radio I listen to for pure enjoyment and not because I couldn't enjoy good radio. I hear things occasionally that just give me a chill—the same chill that sent me into the business. But those moments are few and far between.

Q. *John Steinbeck, in his book* Travels With Charlie, *points out the sameness of radio all over the country. When I traveled I found I had to agree with him. A lot of radio stations play the same music, use the same jingles and have personalities which are interchangeable with each other. You've had the opportunity to see radio from the other side for a while. Do you find the same thing to be true?*

A. When I drove to L.A. from New York and took up living in a new area of the country I expected to hear diversity in radio. I certainly expected the Ozarks and the Blue Ridge mountains to beam music and announcers that reflected the shoveling of the cow barns and the dialogue of Al Capp. Instead of gallons of moonshine, I heard the oozings of Shulke sap. Instead of rotgut country, I heard Burkhart-Abrams and TM Top 40 and AOR standbys. Every market sounded the same—20-30 record playlist, same jingles, announcers who have come from anywhere and end up nowhere . . . or anywhere. Diogenes' real challenge is to find a unique radio station.

Q. *I always prided myself that my station had a very "local" sound. I know your stations did. Were we wrong? Should we have provided the homogenized radio that seems so popular? We both had stations that did well; why did our stations work?*

A. Our stations worked because they were part of their communities. Radio stations are licensed to *serve communities*. If they are to be considered an intimate part of people's lives, they must relate to those people uniquely. I think we were right in making our stations relate and I don't think we can ever lose sight of that aim.

Q. *The hardest thing to me about radio was that it was a seven day a week, 24 hour a day job. When I wasn't at the station or on the air, I was observing* and absorbing background and information I'd use later in programming. I know you worked the same way. What was the hardest thing to you about radio?

A. I think the hardest thing about running a radio station is the terrific time and emotional pressure it places on the PD or GM. The job is timeless, always on call. There's always a crisis in the middle of my vacation. I've never yet spent an entire vacation without at least one crisis-type call. Unlike most businesses, there are no backups for operating personnel on ready call, so when a jock calls in sick (usually five minutes before air time) there's a dilemma. Leave town and you're always worrying, no matter how much has been delegated. Return to town and as soon as you get within signal reach you're straining to hear if the station's on the air and okay. Every time the phone rings, the pit of the stomach churns—what's wrong, who cancelled, oh my God! You drive down the street and every business is a client or a prospect and your mind is back on business. Go shopping and you're selling. Socialize and you're pitching the station. The station's your life because a good station *is* the town in which it's located so your whole life is your work . . . and that's hard work.

Q. *You've had experiences in dealing with the day-to-day finances of radio. The industry is, as a whole, a low-paying one. Do you foresee the day when small and medium market radio people will be paid like professionals in other fields or is the financial picture such as to preclude that possibility?*

A. Unfortunately, I don't see radio performers in small to medium markets being paid proportionally better. The reason is partly that there are more (and always will be more) people looking for jobs than there are openings. The economic law of supply and demand applies. There'll always be a good jock who'll almost pay you for the chance to get a break, and he'll edge out the people who want a good wage.

The other problem is station economics. There are too many radio stations, plus too much other media. Media dollars are getting spread thinner and thinner. Station incomes are going down. Given a choice between raises for the jocks or joining RAB or sending the sales staff through the Jennings Sales Courses, guess which priority instant economics dictates?

Q. *The FCC would like to dramatically increase the number of AM stations available on the band and to make those new facilities available to minority ownership. Without discussing the question of increasing the number of stations itself, I would like to find out from someone who has worked (and sold) small market radio whether you feel the economics structure of most small markets is able to support many new stations.*

A. The idea of adding *more* stations to the spectrum just floors me. In the past two decades we've seen the number of radio stations more than *double* simply by the awareness of the FM band and the splitting of the simulcasting of AM/FM operations. This year's figures indicate a third of America's stations lost money and another third made profits of under $10,000. We can't support new stations. We can't support the ones we have.

Q. *Where do we go from here? What's radio's future?*

A. The media "pie" is cut into many pieces. There's AM radio, FM radio, TV, cable, microwave, video-tape, videodisc, computer banks, print, Telex, and a multitude of other methods of communication. There's a finite audience and the more diverse ways of reaching these people at any given time, logic dictates that the fewer people will be reached by any single medium at that time. The business of radio is facing a great challenge. It can meet this challenge only through creativity, planning, and a realization *now* that the challenge exists.

Q. *If you met someone who wanted to get into radio today, what would be the most valuable piece of advice you could give them?*

A. I would advise that person to be sure he/she understood what he was getting into, and be sure he/she backed themselves with enough educational diversity to have other options if the decision turned out to be the wrong one. If the person persisted, then he/she should follow his instincts as an entertainer, not a scientist, and help rescue a very important form of communication arts.

Index

A
Aging, audience 92-93
Analog recording, 64
Arbitron (ARB) 66, 69-70, 74-90
Audience acceptance, 95-96
   and public interest, 95-96
Audience aging, 92-93
Audience involvement, 17
Audience maintenance, 79-82
Audience rapport, 19-20
Audience turnover, 79-82
Available audience, 85-86
Average Persons, 76
Average Rating, 76

B
Baby boom, 92-93
Balance, Bill, 11
Benny, Jack, 36
Berns, Don, 116-128
Brinkley, David, 18

C
Call-in requests, 59
Candor, 8
C.E. Hooper Company, 66
Communications with GM, 7-8
Competition, 106
Complaints, 100-101
Computers, 107-109
   engineering, 109
   in music programming, 108-109
   in the control room, 109
Contests, 21-23
Contests, costs of, 22
Counseling, 6
Creativity, 10
Cronkite, Walter, 18
Crosby, Bing, 19
Cume, 78
Cume Persons, 78
Cume Rating, 78
Cume ratings, 24-25
Cutouts, 64

D
Daily log, 3-4
Diary survey, 69-71
Digital recording, 64
Disk jockeys, 12-13
Distributor (music), 62
Dubs, 64

E
Education, 9-10
Edwards, Douglas, 18
Efficiency of Target Audience, 82
Entertainment Response Analysis (ERA), 71-72
Established Hits, 33
Exclusive Cume Persons, 78-79
Expanded Sample Frame, 89-90

F
Fear, 107
Firing, 6-7
Free goods, 64

G
General manager, communications with, 7-8
Goals, 107
Godfrey, Arthur, 36
Goldens, 33
Guthrie, Woody, 44

H
"Happy news", 14
Hart, Raymond, 49
Harvey, Paul, 18
Hiring, 4-5
Hitbound, 33
Hot clock, 23-35

I
"Interest, necessity, convenience", 94-96
Interview aided recall survey, 68-69
Interviewing, 5
Investigative journalism, 16-17

J
Jacobs, Frederick, 9

K
King, Jim, 37

L
Landry, Ron, 37
Lifestyle research, 91-92
Lincoln, Murray, 96
Listener activity, 90-91
Localization, 107
Log, daily, 3-4
Lotteries, 96-100
Lottery law, 96-100
   chance, 97
   consideration, 97-99
   prize, 97-98

M
Maintenance, 79-82
Manufacturer (music), 62
Mastering, 64
McCoy, Jack, 51
McMurray, R., 12-13
Metro Share, 77
Metro Survey Area, 87
   Area of Dominant Influence, 87-88
   Designated Marketing Area, 87-88
   Pulse Radio Station Area, 88
   Pulse Special Study Area, 88
   Total Survey Area, 87
Michigan State University, 9
Minorities in broadcasting, 10
Mom & pop store, 63
Money Tree, 97
Monitoring, 2
Monthly commitment check, 4
Mothers, 64
Motivating, 5
Music, 54-65
   formula, 55-57
   research techniques, 57-60
   selection of, 54-55

surveys, 57-60
Music clocks, 31-35
Music rotation, 55-57
Music trade publications, 58

N

Net pricing, 64
News, 13-17
  and audience involvement, 17
  and demographics, 16
  minority, 18
  television, 14
News content, 15
News delivery style, 15
Newsjock, 18-19
Newspaper, relations with, 49-51
Newspapers, 14
News verbiage, 15-16
News writing style, 14-15

O

Off-air positions, 11-12
Off-air promotion, 38-44
  billboards, 38-40
  book covers, 43
  bumper stickers, 42
  bus cards, 40
  coffee cups, 43
  direct mail, 43
  litter boxes, 42
  mail stuffers, 43
  milk carton sides, 43
  newspapers, as promotional tool, 42
  outside appearances, 43
  posters, 43
  telephone, as promotional tool, 43-44
  television, as promotional tool, 40-41
  T-shirts, 43
Ombudsman, 101-102
On-air promotion, 44-52
  Boss Garage, 45
  Car-a-Day Giveaway, 46
  Compassion Line, 46
  Jock in the Box, 44
  Money Phone, 47
  remote broadcasts, 48
  Second Chance Cash, 47
  Treasure Hunt, 46
One-stop, 62
On-scene reporting, 17
Outcall research, 59-60
Overconfidence, 106

P

Patience, 103
Pay scales, 10
Penetration, 78
Personality, 35-37
Personnel functions of PD, 4-7
Persons Using Radio, 75
Pitfalls, 105
Plugola/payola, 54-55
Population, pattern changes of, 92-93
Post-broadcast check, 4
Pre-broadcast check, 4
PR file items, 52-53
Pride, 106-107
Program director, duties of, 2-8
Programming and creativity, iv-v
Programming, as art, iv-vi
Programming, as craft, iv-v
Programming, as science, iv-v
Programming, styles of, 1-2

Programming research, 66-93
Promo copies, 64
Promotion, 38-53
Proposition, 13
Public responsibility, 94-102
Publics, different, 95
Pulse, 66, 68

Q

Quarter hour maintenance, 24-35

R

Rack jobber, 62-63
Rating, 75
Rating surveys, 66-93
Recycling, 83-85
Registration, of slogans, trademarks, etc., 51-52
Relevance, 17
Repetition, 90
Reporting, on-scene, 17
Research, lifestyle, 91-92
Retailer (music), 63
Returns, 64
Roberts, Woody, 20
Rose, Dr. Don, 11
Rotation, music, 55-57

S

Sales, 11
Schlock, 64
Share, 75
Shielding, 6
Shovan, Tom, 45, 146-160
Slogans, 51-52
Smidt, Clark, 134-146
Spot, 24
Spot set/spot break, 24-35
Stamper, 64
Stone, Sebastion, 72
Success, thoughts on, 103-105
Survey areas, 86-89
Swayze, John Cameron, 18
Sweeny, Kevin, 51

T

Talent, 11-12
Target audience, 82-83
Taylor, Gene, 128-130
Telephone coincidental survey, 66-68
Thayer, Jack, 49-51
Time checks, 31
Time Spent Listening, 80
Top 10, 33
Trademarks, 51-52
Training, 5-6
Turnover, 79-82
Turricci, Tom, 72

U

Unit, 24

V

Verbiage, 15-16
Voice, 11
Voicers, 17
Vulnerability, 20

W

Weighting (of diary surveys), 70-71
Whitley, Pat, 46
Winston, Fred, 37
Wolt, Ken (Clayton, Dan), 19, 110-116
Women in broadcasting, 10-11

Y

Young, Terry, 130-134